What Educators Are Saying About The Jewish Educator's Companion

"Writing the book she wishes she always had as an educator, Frankel offers practical applications as well as sound pedagogical theory and background. Taking on subjects many of my teachers tell me they struggle with, from God and *t'filah* to implementing blended learning, this book offers support to Jewish educators at a variety of levels and stages in their careers. She is not afraid to share her mistakes with us, so that we can learn from them as she has. This is a great gift to Jewish educators everywhere."

> — *Rabbi Debbie Young-Somers, Community Educator, Movement for Reform Judaism (UK)*

"*The Jewish Educator's Companion* translates sound educational theory into usable strategies for every Jewish educational setting. Educators can use these tools to introduce critical thinking and Jewish values into their games, projects, and activities. An expert in gaming, filmmaking, and other creative learning strategies, Frankel makes leading educational trends accessible and implementable. If you are seeking a menu of ways to make Jewish learning thoughtful and deep while truly engaging learners, this book is a great guide."

> — *Miriam Heller Stern, Ph.D.,*
> *National Director, School of Education at Hebrew Union College-Jewish Institute of Religion*

"Batsheva Frankel's new book adds something desperately needed in the Jewish educational world—a toolkit to inspire new and veteran teachers alike. We are preparing the next generation of leaders of the Jewish community; we must create an environment that is conducive to that noble goal. With ideas culled from the best of general education and applied to Jewish education, Frankel's work can move the needle in a meaningful way."

> — *Rabbi Ari Segal, Head of School, Shalhevet High School, Los Angeles*

"Batsheva Frankel has given principals a wonderful tool to train their teachers, and given teachers a real understanding of both the theory and practice of Jewish education. These are real educational techniques that can be incorporated into any classroom. Anything that we teach will be taught better now, thanks to this extraordinary guide."

> — *Rabbi Cherie Koller-Fox, President NewCAJE*

"This is an excellent tool for new, as well as seasoned, educators. It breaks down the fundamental aspects of quality learning in a way that is accessible to anyone. This resource is a great combination of theory and application and will guide countless educators through their sacred work."

> — *Rachel Stern, Education Director, Institute for Southern Jewish Life*

"In 2007, the McKinsey report coined the well-known phrase, 'The quality of an education system cannot exceed the quality of its teachers,' and reinforced the importance of investment, empowerment, and development of the most valuable asset of every school—the teachers. In her book, Frankel manages to speak to every teacher, regardless of the age, gender, or geographical location of the students being taught, and to touch on all facets of education—identity and values, school climate, learning methods, curriculum, and evaluation. She does all of this while at the same time relating to the Jewish soul that exists in every Jewish educator."

> — *Dr. Amnon Eldar, Director General of the AMIT Network, Israel*

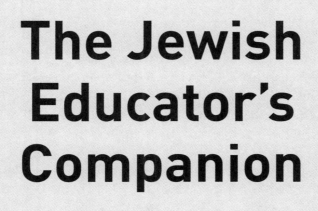

The Jewish Educator's Companion

Practical Tools and Inspirational Ideas

Batsheva Frankel

The publisher wishes to thank the following people, who reviewed an early draft of *The Jewish Educator's Companion*, for their insight and suggestions:
    Lesley Litman
    Evie Rotstein
    Diane Zimmerman

Cover and interior design: Hillel Smith
Editor: Aviva Lucas Gutnick

The publisher gratefully acknowledges the following sources of images:
    Page 71, Shutterstock: StudioSmart (gavel), ergonormal (boots), Preto Perola (vintage sneakers), Elnur (men's shoes), Kenishirotie (men's sneakers), Matryoha (heels), Bplanet (slip-on shoes), Heinz The (Mary Jane shoes), Roman Sigaev (child shoes).

Published by Behrman House, Inc.
11 Edison Place
Springfield, NJ 07081
www.behrmanhouse.com

ISBN 978-0-87441-994-8

Library of Congress Cataloging-in-Publication Data

Names: Frankel, Batsheva, author.
Title: The Jewish educator's companion : practical tools and inspirational
  ideas / Batsheva Frankel.
Description: Springfield, New Jersey : Behrman House, Inc., [2017] | Includes
  bibliographical references.
Identifiers: LCCN 2017012315 | ISBN 9780874419948 (pbk.)
Subjects: LCSH: Jewish students--Religious life--Handbooks, manuals, etc. |
  Jewish religious education--Activity programs.
Classification: LCC BM727 .F65 2017 | DDC 296.6/8--dc23 LC record available at
  https://lccn.loc.gov/2017012315

Printed in the United States of America

This book is dedicated to all of you, the Jewish educators—novice and veteran, part-time and full-time—who are passionately committed to the growth and refining of your craft.

It is also dedicated to the wonderful educators in my past and present, both in the Jewish and secular world, who inspired me and continue to do so:

My third grade teachers—Ms. Kathy Enright, Mrs. Cathy Peterson and Mrs. Dyer—who first showed me how creative teaching and how exciting learning could be (all without computers or even copy machines).

My fifth grade Hebrew school teacher, Cantor Maurice Weiss.

A few of my many great teachers at Cherry Creek High School—
Mr. Mark Hampshire, Mr. Ralph Remmes, Mr. Mike Prevedal,
Mrs. Paulette Wasserstein.

All of the mentors and inspirational colleagues I've had in my teaching career, including (but not limited to) Ellen Howard, Rabbi Leah Kroll, Jim Hahn, and the incredible teachers at Arete Preparatory Academy.

Table of Contents

Introduction

This is the book that I wish I'd had during my first year of teaching. And my fifth year. And my fifteenth. If you want a guide that speaks to you with both practical advice and discussion of why things work, whether you are a novice educator, a veteran, or somewhere in-between, this book is for you.

There are many kinds of Jewish educators: congregational and day-school teachers and administrators, youth group leaders and facilitators, consultants and specialists; freelance, part-time, full-time. Many of us have worn more than one hat, and continue to. This book was written for all of us engaged in this special calling known as Jewish education.

Many professional development books in the secular education world are primarily philosophy. Over the years, I've expanded my vision by reading books by educators such as Sir Ken Robinson and Alfie Kohn. I always thought it would be great if there were a practical version of their books that offered concrete tools and examples for me to use. Other career-changing texts I've read or conferences and workshops I've attended on methodologies like Understanding by Design and Project Based Learning transformed my teaching. But those examples are primarily for math, science, and, occasionally, language arts or social studies. I wanted to translate that learning into a book or workshop with real tools and solid ideas, lessons and practical examples for my *Tanach*, Jewish history, or other Judaic-studies classes. I also wanted to hear how the different educational philosophies and methodologies apply to my curriculum. I wanted a little bit of solid educational philosophy and a lot of practical tools to use right away. This is that book.

Treat this book like a giant workshop designed to help you engage your students and make your classroom come alive. It's filled with all of the tools, methodologies, activities, ideas, and techniques that I have developed, learned, and used throughout my career as a Jewish educator.

The heart of this book is material I have developed and used in workshops, teacher-training events, and classrooms. Each chapter feels like a mini-workshop: Scan the table of contents and see which chapters would be most useful to you, which workshops you would like to "attend." Start with those.

Part One is devoted to improving our students' critical thinking and analytical abilities. These are big-picture skills that all Jewish educators can appreciate. Learn about three solid methodologies to help students grow these important skills.

Part Two explores a Jewish twist on STEM, which focuses on how to introduce concepts such as spirituality and ethics, or reinforce them in learning spaces.

Part Three delves into some methodologies and techniques that are changing or enhancing traditional education, such as Understanding by Design and Flipped Learning. As you explore each one, consider which might strengthen your curriculum.

Part Four moves into the learning space with practical suggestions, activities, and templates to help with everything from building a community, to managing a classroom, to creating a lesson plan.

Lastly, Part Five, written with school directors and principals in mind, provides a practical process for approaching change, whether large or small, and inspirational examples of innovative educational programs from all kinds of communities.

Just as some workshops are five-hour intensives and others are a packed hour or two, the chapters here vary in length. Some chapters have templates at the end that you can use. Others invite participation and interaction with the material as you reflect on questions. Each chapter is meant to inspire you.

Because one of the biggest strengths of a workshop (versus a lecture) is its collaborative nature, you'll notice in this book a few other educators' stories, called "Celebrating Success." As you experiment with the content in this book, or if you have your own lessons or ideas that might inspire others, make sure to share with your colleagues. In this way, we are all participating together and learning from each other, which strengthens not only our own practices, but Jewish education as a whole.

Ready for our first workshop? Pick one and dig in!

NOTE

Organic learning can include the occasional digression, surprising insight, moment of silent contemplation, and so on. Therefore, you won't find suggested answers to any discussion questions in this book. What I've learned over the years is that no conversation ever goes the same way twice, and that's what I love about education.

PART ONE

Developing Critical Thinking Skills

A colleague of mine was visiting a friend, whose ten-year-old daughter interrupted their conversation. "Mom, what's 12 times 14?" She and her little brother were engaged in a project and needed the information. My teacher colleague immediately jumped in. "Well, what's 10 times 14?" The girl's face flashed annoyance, quickly replaced by a look of concentration. Clearly pleased with herself, she said, "140!" Just as the teacher asked the girl to calculate 2 times 14 so she could add it to the 140, her mom blurted out, "168." Smartphone in hand, the mom said proudly, "I just used the calculator." Her daughter said "thanks" and ran off. The teacher's heart sank; an opportunity for learning had just been missed.

People often engage in what I call a "Google education"—wanting instant answers without having to search too much. The good news is that we have vast amounts of information at our fingertips. The flip side is trying to sift through and analyze all of this information critically. Do we lose something when the answers are so easy to find, basically given to us? Where or how does Judaism fit in?

Because we want our students to find meaning in and connection to their Judaism at a time when there is so much competition for their attention, it is important to expose students to deeper understandings of Judaism using their critical-thinking skills. We can help do this through the ancient Jewish tradition of questioning. When students are comfortable enough to ask their own questions and analyze sources (text, commentaries, the views of teachers and fellow students), they engage intellectually and emotionally with the material, and more readily find relevance in the content and joy in the process—essential goals of Jewish education. And it helps if it's fun. Additionally, using games and a technique called Text Activators to increase critical-thinking skills open up doors to learning for all students, not just those who are good readers or who can easily participate in discussions. This section explores some powerful ways to engage students and exercise their brains.

Good Questions Are the Answer ▶ **1**
Lenses of Questioning

I always knew the value of teaching my students to ask good questions. When we would study Torah, I would say to them, "Okay, ask me a question about the text." Often I could hear the crickets chirping as the silence in the room told me that perhaps I was too vague in my request. Then I tried having students "write down three good questions," thinking that perhaps they were too shy to ask their questions out loud. The majority of the questions they would write down were basic comprehension questions, because that is what they thought I was asking for. I realized that if I wanted them to learn to ask strong, analytical questions, I would have to first model this skill for them, helping them hone their own critical-thinking skills.

As educators, we know that Judaism can help our students navigate their lives, and, of course, we want them to understand why leading a Jewish life is meaningful. If we start the process of helping them explore the depths of Judaism early on, then by the time they get to college, they will know there is more to Judaism than just stories and holidays. We can best offer this opportunity to our students by both modeling for them and teaching them how to ask great questions.

◈ A Little Educational Philosophy

The ancient Jewish tradition of questioning teaches the skill of thoughtful, critical inquiry. Dan Rothstein and Luz Santana explain in *Make Just One Change: Teach Students to Ask Their Own Questions* that, "if we want to stimulate students' curiosity or engage them more effectively . . . teaching students to ask their own questions can accomplish these same goals while teaching a critical lifelong skill."[1]

Traditional Jewish learning focuses on questions, showing us that good questions are the answer to real learning. We see it when we study Talmud, Halachah, or any Jewish text. Rashi's commentaries, for example, are almost always answers to his questions about the text. In fact, there are many different kinds of queries that can help us acquire knowledge and analyze data. Often, as educators and learners, we lean heavily on only one kind of questioning, without even realizing it. If our students can connect to that type of question, then they might answer it. But typically in a class discussion, only a few students actively participate. Often, students' learning styles dictate the type of question they gravitate toward, which may or may not match the teacher's style of questioning. The more we as teachers understand and model using different categories of inquiry, the better we can train our and our students' minds to explore every facet of a topic or idea. This leads to students' deeper critical-thinking skills and imaginative observations. Such skills are crucial to our students as they explore Jewish texts, rituals, and philosophical and theological ideas in an increasingly mature fashion, and as they discover and solidify their Jewish identity. Additionally, as our students navigate through the world with its various challenges, choices, and dilemmas, we want them to feel prepared to ask good questions that will lead to a smoother and more fulfilling journey.

◆ Practical Tools

A surefire approach for training students to ask and analyze strong questions is the Lenses of Questioning method. It's loosely based on a business model used in group planning called Six Thinking Hats.[2] Generally speaking, all questions fall into six categories, each with its own purpose:

1. **Factual:** Questions that are closed-ended and include data-driven, facts-oriented, and informational inquiries.

2. **Big Picture:** Questions that concern themes, goals, processes, and summaries.

3. **Creative:** Questions that ask about alternatives and creative interpretations. A popular opening for this kind of question is "What if...?"

4. **Beneficial:** Questions that focus on positive thinking, including best scenarios, benefits, and optimistic outcomes.

5. **Cautionary:** Questions that examine weaknesses, risks, and potential problems.

6. **Emotional:** Questions that deal with feelings, the impact on others, or fears or intuitions.

THE LENSES OF QUESTIONING

Now, imagine that each category corresponds to a different colored lens that can help focus our questioning. Using this symbolic framework can help us think clearly and thoroughly in a concentrated direction. By thinking in these terms, each of us can expand our portfolio of question-asking approaches beyond those with which we are already comfortable. Additionally, by learning to determine the kinds of questions asked, students will gain valuable practice in critical thinking and analytical skills.

This chapter explores how to use this fun and easy system. Let's see how the colors of the lenses correspond to the six types of questions.

ORANGE • Facts

Questions that explore
Information
Data
Facts

YELLOW • Benefits

Questions that explore
Best scenarios
Optimism
Positive thinking

BLUE • Big Picture

Questions that explore
Focus and themes
Process
Summary
Objective

GRAY • Cautions

Questions that explore
Risks
Potential problems
Weaknesses

GREEN • Creativity

Questions that explore
Alternative solutions
Creative thinking
What if...?

RED • Emotions

Questions that explore
Feelings
Fears
Impact on others
Intuition

NOTE

To determine the color lens of a question, consider only the question, not the answer. For example, let's look at the question, "What impact does tzedakah have on the giver?" You might be tempted to call it a "yellow-lens" question because the answer might be about the benefits. But it is actually a "red-lens" question, because it's about impact, which could include unbeneficial ramifications. Another example: "What if no one gave tzedakah?" This might seem like a grey question because the results might be problematic, but it's really a green question because it asks a "what if" question that forces creative thinking. Having students debate the categories of questions helps them develop analytical skills as they think through every angle of an issue, which also leads them to think more deeply about the answers.

HOW TO GET STARTED

To familiarize students with this approach, first model the different kinds of questions. Give each student a copy of the chart. Consider putting a copy on the wall. Then, while introducing a piece of text, concept, idea, prayer, or story, ask different questions about your topic while prefacing each question with an explanation about its lens color.

For example, if the topic is tzedakah, and you want to ask, "Why is giving tzedakah important?" tell your students that you will be asking a blue-lens question, and explain that the blue lens focuses on themes and objectives. Next, you might ask, "How does it make you feel when you give tzedakah or help someone in need?" First explain that this is a red-lens question because it deals with feelings.

Depending on the age of the students, you might ask your next question, and let them see if they can figure out the category and tell you why.

You can take this strategy to a higher level by using actual colored lenses as visual cues. (A template for creating your own mock glasses is available at the end of this chapter, or you can find a link to a complete kit that includes glasses with different colored lenses at www.behrmanhouse.com/jec.) Younger students, in particular, often find it helpful if you wear the glasses while asking the questions. After students begin to understand the Lenses of Questioning concept, ask them to identify which color lens should be worn for each question you ask.

Let's look at how the different color questions work with an example about Rosh Hashanah:

1. **Orange Question:** *In what Hebrew month is Rosh Hashanah?*
   This is fact based. Students know that even if they don't know the answer, they can look it up.

2. **Blue Question:** *What is the purpose of Rosh Hashanah?*
   This is a blue question because it deals with the themes, agenda, and bigger picture of the holiday, and is thus a larger question to discuss and debate. Students could research it first, if they needed to, and then bring back what they've learned to the discussion. As an open-ended question, it may have more than one answer.

3. **Green Question:** *What new traditions would you add to celebrating Rosh Hashanah?*
   This is a green question because it requires imagination and creative thinking.

4. **Yellow Question:** *What are the benefits of new beginnings?*
   This is a yellow question because it deals with positive thinking and benefits.

5. **Gray Question:** *What are the challenges of starting over?*
   This is a gray question because it deals with weaknesses, challenges, and potential risks.

6. **Red Question:** What does Rosh Hashanah mean to you?
   This is a red question because it deals with emotions and impact.

THE NEXT STEP: STUDENTS GENERATE QUESTIONS

When introducing a piece of text, a concept, idea, prayer, or story, here are some suggestions to generate analytical thinking and questions:

- Assign each student, pair, or group of students (depending on the size of your class) a different color lens and have them write down as many questions for their lens color as possible in ten minutes. When students present their questions to the class, have the class evaluate whether their questions really fit the assigned category. Then have each student, pair, or

TIP

Just as you model for the students the different kinds of questions, let them pick from the glasses and wear the lenses for questions they ask as well. Older students may not need the physical glasses, but some might enjoy it. You know your students.

group pass the questions around to see who will answer them. This can be done as a round-robin, with participants handing their questions to the left, taking five minutes to answer the questions they received, and then passing to the left again, until all of the questions have been answered.

- Have students, on their own, in pairs, or in groups, try to generate six questions, one for each color lens. If they are in pairs or groups, they can debate and refine together before presenting. If they are working on their own, they can swap lists with another student to discuss, compare, and refine each other's work. Decide if or how you want students to try to answer some or all of the questions. Having students evaluate which kinds of questions were easier for them to form, and which were more challenging, adds a level of self-reflection to the activity that helps students become invested in their learning.

- **For students in grades K through 2:** Ask students to help you come up with two questions for each lens color. Write the questions for each lens color on a giant Post-it Note and hang the notes around the room. Ask students to stand by the questions they would most like to answer. Then go around the room and have students answer those questions.

- **For students in grade 3 and above:** Introduce a piece of text, such as the story of Noah and the Ark or the Twelve Spies who enter Canaan on a scouting mission. Divide students into groups of two or three, and have them review the text. Assign each group a different lens color and tell them to generate six questions for that color lens. Mill about and assist them if they are unsure whether a particular question truly fits into their assigned category. Let them debate it and refine the question if necessary.

  Then hang six giant Post-it Notes around the room, one for each lens, and give each group a colored marker that matches their assigned lens color. Ask each group to pick their two favorite questions and write them on their Post-it Note, one question at the top of the page and one toward the middle (to leave room for answers!). After students have completed these tasks, do one of two things:

  Have students answer any of the questions they want, whether from their own group or others, with a purple or brown marker (since those are not lens colors). Then others can comment on the answers, beginning a written dialogue. This is a great way to make sure that all students get a chance to "speak." This method works best with middle-school and high-school students. After all of the students have finished engaging with the questions, a representative from each group can share their group's Post-it Note "discussion."

  Or, go around and read the questions, seeing where they take you. For example, if students asking a red-lens question wrote, "What were the spies feeling as they entered Canaan?" you might ask the class to take ten minutes and write skits that explore that question. If the green-lens group asked, "What would have happened if the spies had all come back with an enthusiastic report?" students can speculate in groups and present their answers.

When students' questions are used as the springboard for further learning and examination, students become more invested in the lesson.

ADVANCING UNDERSTANDING

When students feel comfortable with the lens categories, turn any session into a critical-thinking game. To engage and inspire students, or as an assessment, use the following games with the Lenses of Questioning die (part of the complete kit available at behrmanhouse.com/jec, or make your own using the template at the end of this chapter; more about making and using games in chapter 2).

Game 1: Assign each person, pair, or group a lens color, and have them generate five to ten written questions, which they will fold and stack next to the appropriate colored glasses. Then, taking turns, each student rolls the die. The color on the die determines which question pile the student will pick from. Students must first make sure that the questions truly belong in the categories into which they've been placed. If they judge a question to be correctly placed, the person or team that wrote the question earns a point. If the student who rolled the die answers the question well (most questions don't have a "right" answer, but students should evaluate whether it was a thoughtful or supported answer), the student or team also gets a point.

Game 2: Each student generates one or two written questions for each color lens and puts them in bags (one bag per color) or in piles by their corresponding glasses. Each student rolls the die, then picks a question from the corresponding bag or pile. If they determine that the question belongs in a different category, they can move the question to its correct category and pick a new question, or they can choose to fix the question so that it works in its original category. Students get a point for each question they answer correctly and a bonus point for fixing a question.

Variation: After students write and sort the questions into piles according to color, divide the class into two or three teams. Each team rolls the die three or four times, and then has to answer a question from each of the corresponding color piles within a fixed amount of time, such as two minutes. For example, a team that rolls one blue, one green, and one yellow would have two minutes total to answer three questions as a team.

It's possible that students would have to answer more than one question from a particular color pile if, for example, they roll two red and one orange. Award points for all the questions they answer well.

Game 3: This game is for advanced students. As a topic or text is introduced, have students take turns rolling the die and generating a question from the corresponding lens category. Award a point for successfully creating a question that truly fits the category and a point to any student who answers the question.

Variation: Working in *chevruta* (learning pairs), have one student roll the die and come up with a question from that color category for the partner to answer. Then switch roles and repeat the process. Students could also discuss or debate together. Setting a time limit for this activity—fifteen minutes, for example—gives a sense of urgency. Gather students together afterward to share what they have learned from each other.

• • •

Use this methodology of asking questions strategically throughout the year. Not only will students begin to ask richer questions, their answers will be more thoughtful and creative. Previously unreachable students, who might space out during a typical question-and-answer period (teacher-generated questions for students to answer), will connect to both the material and the class as their own questions get answered. As teachers, we can also challenge ourselves to ask questions differently, in a way that can help us connect to more students. As students begin asking better questions, they will also become more invested and interested in what they are learning.

Make Your Own Lenses of Questioning

Lenses: Copy the template onto colored construction paper (using the colors of the lenses) or copy it onto white card stock and have students color in the frames for each category. Add plastic lenses if desired.

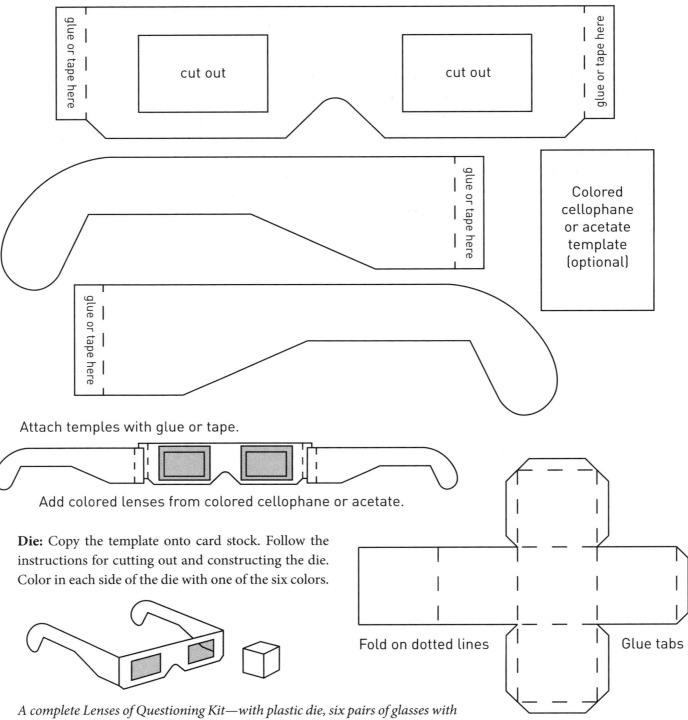

Die: Copy the template onto card stock. Follow the instructions for cutting out and constructing the die. Color in each side of the die with one of the six colors.

A complete Lenses of Questioning Kit—with plastic die, six pairs of glasses with colored lenses, and directions—is available at behrmanhouse.com/jec.

Real Game Changers ▶2

Critical-Thinking Games

When I was a student in Hebrew school (as it was called back then), we played "Hollywood Squares," a TV tic-tac-toe game show with celebrities in each square, to help reinforce our Hebrew reading skills. Mrs. Amitai would rearrange all the desks to emulate the show's setup, and we rotated roles—some students played the celebrities and two people were the contestants. Mrs. Amitai was always the host, of course. She would hold up a Hebrew word, and a contestant would ask a celebrity to pronounce it. If the contestant agreed that the celebrity said it correctly, and he or she was right, the contestant could put an X or an O on that "square." Many years later, I still remember how fun it was to learn Hebrew in a way that also made me think. The game was exciting to my eight-year-old self, but also effective in a way I didn't appreciate until I became a teacher. The benefits to me as a learner lasted.

When I started teaching, I realized that games were more than just fun—they were excellent tools for facilitating and assessing learning. Instead of just making up games for my students, though, I teach my students how to create games that involve using, and therefore strengthening, critical-thinking skills.

Many creative teachers understand instinctually that learning through games is not only valid but crucial in congregational schools. There are many kinds of games, and the ones that train our students to use critical thinking and analytical skills don't all involve rearranging the furniture or having students run around. There are thinking games, puzzles, board games, and more in this chapter. The key to creating and using games to their fullest potential lies with our ability to fashion games that in every way reflect the lessons we are trying to convey. Educating our students to create games helps them own the material they are learning and empowers them to teach others.

⬢ A Little Educational Philosophy

What is it about playing games that helps facilitate learning? Why is this methodology especially important today?

More than ever, the value of game playing in our educational system has taken root. In fact, organizations such as the Institute of Play herald the educational gains of game playing beyond entertainment value and have put game playing at the center of their school curriculum, not as an add-on, but as the primary means for facilitating and integrating information.

The Institute of Play created the innovative Quest Schools, run by a group of game designers and classroom teachers. Together they set out to engage and empower students by using game design and systems thinking as the basis for the schools' pedagogical approach. Their first school, Quest to Learn, in Brooklyn, pioneered the idea of using complex challenges, in the form of various games, so learners could interact with content in an exciting and relevant way. Quest's success has led to more schools and learning programs across the country using games to facilitate higher-level learning.

In *Why Games and Learning*, the founders of the Institute of Play state, "Many experts believe that success in the 21st century depends on education that treats higher order skills, like the ability to think, solve complex problems or interact critically through language and media. Games naturally support this form of education."[1]

We are not talking here about Jewpardy or Rosh Hashanah Chutes and Ladders (although both can be fun), but about a whole different way of looking at games that involves higher-order thinking, assimilation of ideas, complex challenges, and relatable content presented in an engaging package.

There are three core types of educational games:

1. **Teaching Games** that introduce and teach new material.

2. **Reviewing** or **Reinforcing Games** about previously introduced material.

3. **Assessment Games** to gauge students' knowledge and/or understanding of material.

Most games that truly promote critical thinking and analytical skills fall into the first two categories. Asking students to *create* a game as an assessment, which is the third category, really exercises their brains because they have to show a deeper understanding of the learned information. In addition, if the goal is to assess students' knowledge (also see chapter 15), teacher-developed games can help learners analyze and assimilate information as they are being appraised.

⬡ Practical Tools

Years ago, after talking with and teaching many teens who wanted to address important questions about life, I searched for activities that focused on these matters from a Jewish perspective. Not satisfied with what was out there, I created a few of my own activities and discovered how games can be powerful teaching tools. I'll walk you through the step-by-step process of creating a game for any topic. Then you'll see how I applied those steps to create something called Feed Your Wolves, which helps students understand how the inclination toward doing good (*yetzer hatov*) and the inclination toward doing evil (*yetzer hara*) work in us and the world.

For effective game design, every aspect of the game should align with the ideas or lessons you are trying to express. Use the following process and blank game-creation template (found at the end of this chapter) to develop a successful critical-thinking game.

NINE STEPS TO CREATING ANY GAME

Step 1. Consider the themes, big ideas, or learning objectives of the game.
This part is crucial: Just as in quality lesson planning, games should reflect your big-picture goals.

Step 2. Think about what skills and knowledge you want your players to acquire or to have reinforced.
These can be content based, like *t'filah* skills, or they can be 21st century classroom skills like collaboration, cooperation, and analysis. Knowledge includes understanding content, events, Torah stories, and other topics.

Step 3. Choose a format.
Weigh all of your objectives, think about the materials you have on hand (or what you can buy or create, if you have a budget), and try to match the game type to your purposes. There are many different kinds of games, each with its own educational strengths. Later in the chapter, you'll find examples for each of the following game formats:

- Board games
- Simulation games
- Physical games
- Card games
- Game shows

As you are brainstorming, look around for inspiration: What games do you love? What games do your students love? What would be fun? Most importantly, what format would best suit your needs?

After you've chosen your basic format, it's time to work on the details. The next steps can happen in any order.

Step 4. Decide what element(s) you will use to convey your idea.

Elements can include board, cards, video, ball, ball court, dice, spinner, etc. Each element should clearly reflect your idea (see Sample Game Design: Creating Feed Your Wolves below for an example).

Step 5. Choose what game pieces to use.

Whether you use tokens, markers, or other pieces, consider how they will reflect your idea.

Step 6. Determine the game objective.

This should clearly relate to your lesson, theme, big idea, or learning objectives.

Step 7. Choose the number of players.

How many players will be able to participate at one time? There are many considerations, such as:

- Who is your audience?
- Will the game require teams?
- Do you want participants to compete against each other or work together?
- What is the minimum number of participants it would take to make the game work?
- What is the maximum number of players before it becomes ineffective?

Step 8. Create the game rules.

The clearer and more detailed you are, the better the game will be. Don't forget to include how the game ends.

Step 9. Gather your supplies.

What will you need to make this work? Can you find all the items you need? Do you need to create them yourself? Will you need to have items made? What is your budget?

Ready, set, go! Create your game. Let your imagination run and have fun.

You can also teach your students to make their own games using these steps. I have sometimes asked my students at the end of the scholastic year to create a game that expresses their favorite lesson from the year. It is a wonderful assessment and also reinforces what we learned throughout the year as students play each other's games.

Sample Game Design: Creating Feed Your Wolves

Let's look at how I used these nine steps to create a game. This game explores Jewish ideas about how good and evil might work in the world. It uses cards and a die to facilitate challenges and discussions as all of the players work together to symbolically bring light into the world to win the game.

Step 1. Consider the themes, big ideas, or learning objectives of the game.

I want students to explore these ideas:

- The inclination for good and not-so-good resides in us all.
- There are ramifications to the choices we make, including how those choices can affect the world.
- When we make choices using our good inclination, we bring more light into the world.

Step 2. Think about what skills and knowledge you want your players to acquire or to have reinforced.

I want students to analyze and reflect on various ways the good inclination and evil inclination work in us. I also want students to collaborate with each other, as well as engage in self-reflection.

Step 3. Choose a format.

I was inspired by watching my students play card and dice games like Magic: The Gathering. I wanted to try something that primarily used cards to determine what happens. I remembered the following story, and thought it was a perfect actualization of how the good and evil inclinations work:

> One evening, an elderly Cherokee told his grandson about a battle that goes on inside all people. He said, "My son, the battle is between two 'wolves' inside us all. One is evil. It is anger, envy, jealousy, sorrow, regret, greed, arrogance, self-pity, guilt, resentment, inferiority, lies, false pride, superiority, and ego.
>
> "The other is good. It is joy, peace, love, hope, serenity, humility, kindness, benevolence, empathy, generosity, truth, compassion, and faith."
>
> The grandson thought for a minute and then asked his grandfather, "Which wolf wins?"
>
> The old man replied simply, "The one that you feed."

Once I had this image in my head of two wolves that represent the good and evil inclinations, I conceived of a game that would give players challenges to determine whether their good wolf or bad wolf got fed.

Step 4. Decide what element(s) you will use to convey your idea.

I wanted to use cards, giving each player his or her own good inclination wolf card and evil inclination wolf card. I also needed cards that helped determine the action—which wolves were fed, and how students would be exposed to and interact with different ideas on my subject. I also wanted a unique die (to conjure up images of other role-playing games students might be familiar with) for some of the action, so I purposely picked a die with Arabic numerals instead of the standard dots. I created a deck of cards that contained:

- five sets of "Good Wolf" and "Evil Wolf" cards
- three different kinds of "Action" cards that determined which wolves get fed
- seven "Darkness" cards and seven "Light" cards

Step 5. Choose what game pieces to use.

I wanted to symbolize snacks to feed the wolves and chose small green plastic bingo chips ($48 for 10,000 chips!).

Step 6. Determine the game objective.

Every time a player gets five snacks for their good-inclination wolf, the whole group turns over a "Light" card, because the good inclination brings light into the world. When a person gets five snacks for their evil-inclination wolf, the whole group turns over a "Darkness" card, because the evil inclination brings darkness to the world. The object of the game is for the whole group to turn over all of the "Light" cards before all of the "Darkness" cards are turned over. When that happens, the whole group (representing our world!) wins. This reflects two of the understandings I wanted to convey:

- There are ramifications to the choices we make, including how those choices can affect the world.
- When we make choices from our good inclination, we bring more light into the world.

Step 7. Choose the number of players.

After much deliberation, I decided that two to five players would create the richest experience for everybody. When I use the game with classes or larger groups, I rotate it in a station with other activities that deal with the concepts of good and evil, or bring several Feed Your Wolf games and divide players into small groups.

Step 8. Create the game rules.

Be as clear as possible. In this game, I included the story of the two battling wolves to provide context.

Step 9. Gather your supplies.

I needed a deck of cards. Creating and printing them on your computer works fine if you aren't making many sets. There are many companies and teacher supply stores that sell game supplies, such as dice and plastic tokens, in various quantities.

GAME FORMATS

As you look at some of the examples in each category, think about how you might adapt them to your particular curriculum and goals or age group. Let them inspire your own imagination.

Board Games

Board games offer students opportunities to express knowledge, and they are a popular choice for student-created games. Every part of the game, from the shape of the board (which can even be three-dimensional), to the tokens, to any of the other game elements, creates chances to reflect the ideas that students want to convey.

When I taught seventh grade, students ended each school year by choosing one unit and creating a board game to show their understanding of the lesson, while reinforcing it for the other students playing the game. Here are two of my best student-created games:

Guard Your Tongue Game (*Type: Assessment/Review; grades 5-8*) The board was in the shape of a mouth, with players moving in spaces created on the lips. The mouth was open, and a three-dimensional tongue came out that held cards describing typical middle-school situations. Players had to decide whether each situation was gossip or not, based on the Jewish laws regarding *lashon hara* (gossip or evil speech) that they had learned. If they were right, they moved forward; wrong and they were held back by a guard. The first person to get to the inside of the mouth won.

Jewish Leaders Game (*Type: Assessment/Review; grades 5-8*) Each player had a token that was either Moses, Aaron, Miriam, Sampson, Jonah, or Deborah (the different people we had studied). Everyone started together on a board that looked like a race track, with each player in a starting position. Each player took turns picking cards that had different qualities or traits on them, such as "beloved by everyone," "humble," or "great judge of character." If the leader on the player's token could lay claim to that quality or trait, and the player could support the statement, the player moved ahead. The goal of the game was to reflect the understanding that there are many kinds of Jewish leaders, each with many important characteristics.

Here are two examples of educator-created board games:

On the Road Again (*Type: Teaching; grades 3 and up*) In this game about *t'shuvah*, returning to our truest positive self, the board is a path through many obstacles that might sidetrack players. Every time players land on an obstacle, they pick a card that describes how they went off the path (what they did wrong). Players have thirty seconds to explain how they would fix it, using one of the ideas about *t'shuvah* they have studied. If they are successful, they are allowed back on the path. (This can also be created as a physical game, as you will see on page 26).

Jewish Holidays (*Type: Assessment/Review; any age*) The board is shaped like a circle (the Jewish year). As players move around the board using a spinner, they have a chance to land on a holiday. Each holiday takes up as many spaces as the holiday is long. For example, Rosh Hashanah is two days long, so it takes up two spaces, giving players two chances to land on it. Shabbat squares are sprinkled throughout. Each time a player lands on a holiday, he or she answers a question about it. If a player answers correctly, he or she collects one of three tokens that represent that holiday (i.e., a matzah, shank bone, or frog for Pesach). The first player to collect all three tokens from three different holidays/Shabbat wins the game. This game works for any age, depending on the difficulty and sophistication of the questions, whether written by the teacher or students.

Simulation Games

Simulation games, almost always teaching games, are particularly great for Jewish history and can have a strong impact on participants because they offer an opportunity to appreciate another point of view or experience. A simulation game differs from an activity aimed at understanding a concept in that there is some kind of objective participants work to achieve.

Russian Jewry Game *(Type: Teaching; grades 8-12)* Based on the ideas in educator Elissa Blaser's Exodus: The Russian Jewry Simulation Game, which was widely played in the 1970s and 1980s. The original is challenging to find, but you can create something similar as described below.

Object: Help students understand the modern Exodus miracle that occurred when the Jewish people came together on behalf of fellow Jews refused permission to emigrate from the Soviet Union in the 1970s and 1980s. After playing, show the documentary *Refusenik*, directed by Laura Bialis, to solidify the experience and give students a glimpse into this important, yet often overlooked, time in Jewish history.

How to play: In this simulation, everyone has a role to play, from Soviet government workers, to Jews trying to escape. The participants simulate going through the challenging process faced by Soviet Jews—visiting various offices to get exit visas, being harassed, and so on. For more details, see *Managing the Jewish Classroom: How to Transform Yourself into a Master Teacher* by Seymour Rossel.[2] With a little bit of research, you can recreate a version of this game, or even have your students create it for other learners. They can generate roles for participants based on what they discover about the challenges of the Refuseniks.

Converso Shabbat *(Type: Teaching; grades 5-8)* Conversos were "hidden" Jews, Jews who claimed to be Christian during the time of the Inquisition but who practiced their Judaism in secret. This game simulates a converso Shabbat.

Object: Often when we learn about historical events, we don't really connect to them on an emotional level. However, personalizing the experience allows learners to connect with our Jewish past in a more concrete way. The object of this simulation is to bring to life the challenges faced by conversos during the last centuries of the Middle Ages. Learners can experience not only the commitment of converso Jews, but also the intense dangers they faced as they tried to remain Jewish in private.

How to play: After learning the basics about conversos, tell students they are going to be having a secret converso Shabbat celebration. Tell everyone the secret location (any room in which the windows have been blacked out, decorated to look like a Spartan Shabbat hideout). Students must find their way there without getting caught. Prearrange for two students to act as leaders, and let them know what will happen. After all students manage to find their way to the secret location, the two student leaders will conduct Shabbat services. This will be interrupted by the grand inquisitor (played by someone who is intimidating and perhaps unknown to the students), who will take the two leaders away. Participants, who believe they've "won" the game because they got to the room safely to enjoy Shabbat, suddenly realize that they were still in great danger by celebrating together. After the simulation, it is important to have students remain in character and process the game as a group or in their journals.

Going to America *(Type: Teaching; grades 3-6)* Every Jewish person in America has family that came from somewhere else. The challenge for these immigrants has always been trying to find harmony between their identity and their adaptation to their new country.

Object: To balance the excitement of immigrating to America from other countries with the challenge of retaining one's native culture and Jewish identity.

How to play: Divide students into "families" of three, four, or five members. Each person in the family gets a (teacher-created) role card.

Each family should come up with a list of ten items—eight Jewish and/or personal objects, plus two items that will remind them of their native culture—that they would like to take with them. These can be actual items or photographs copied onto large index cards or construction paper with descriptions on the back. For example:

ITEM	BACKGROUND
Menorah	Passed down in family for many generations.
Beautifully painted wooden dreidel	A gift to the kids from their favorite uncle. They always played dreidel with him on Chanukah.
Seder plate	Used at every Pesach seder and is over one hundred years old.
Shabbat candlesticks	An heirloom passed down to the mom from her great-grandmother.
Shabbat candlesticks	Given as a gift to the daughter from her grandmother.
Silver tzedakah box	The family puts money in it every week and gives it to the poor of their town.
Siddur	This has been in the family for more than fifty years.
A cookbook of native foods	This collection of handwritten recipes, handed down over many years, includes both dishes from their home country and traditional Jewish foods from their culture.
A large, expensive doll	Dressed in the native costume of their country.
Hamsa	A hand-shaped amulet for warding off the evil eye.

Give each family their immigration papers (below) and fifteen minutes to pick five items from their list. They will have to discuss with family members which are the most important items to pack, since there is not room to take them all.

Afterward, have families present their items and explain them to the customs official (which can be you, another adult, or some students) at Ellis Island, trying to convince the official to let each item in because of its importance. The goal is to get all five items into America.

NOTE

Fill in the immigration paper for each family before you hand it to them. The date should correspond to times people might have immigrated here. For example, a Jewish family from Germany might have come in the mid-1800s, while a Jewish family from Poland might have come in the early 1900s. An Iranian Jewish family might have come in the late 1970s, and a Russian Jewish family might have come in the late 1980s or early '90s. Older students can research what it was like for the Jews of that country and what the journey might have been like to get to America (boat or airplane, through other countries, etc.). Include that information for younger students, and possibly show them a video.

United States of America Immigration Form

Name _____

Country of Origin _____ Date _____

Destination _____
                                               CITY   STATE

Names and Ages of Family Members _____

_____

_____

Items you are declaring _____

_____

Official's signature _____

Physical Games

A physical game allows students to move around and have an experience, but with more of a competitive aspect to it than a simulation game (see chapter 11 for more on experiential learning). Whereas simulations involve some sort of role-playing, physical games don't have to.

The board game On the Road Again can, for example, be transformed into a physical game by creating an actual obstacle course, with each player trying to get past the obstacle to return to the path (doing *t'shuvah*). Make the metaphor as sophisticated as your students can handle.

Escape from Egypt *(Type: Teaching/Review/Assessment; grades 3-12)* A breakout game can be an exciting way to combine physicality with puzzle solving or quiz questions. In this game, players try to leave a designated area (Egypt) by answering challenging Pesach questions, which lead to clues for other questions. If students have been learning about the Exodus, they can solve puzzles that deal with ideas or commentaries that they have studied.

CELEBRATING SUCCESS

Brainstorming ideas with fellow educators can help you create games fast. The collaborative process can help you think through details, as well as look at the big picture. You can help each other stay on track and make sure that the game truly reflects the overall goals.

Thanks to Janiece Gratch, Dvora Kravitz, Tamar Shulman, and Steven Walvick, who created these game ideas in less than an hour with me at a workshop in 2016.

Secret Code Spy Game *(Type: Teaching; grades 1-4)* The goal of this game is to help students work on Hebrew decoding skills while giving them a fun learning incentive.

How to play: Students, competing in teams of three or four, play spies. The teacher creates a mission in the form of a treasure hunt. For example, the spies might look for the location of a secret formula and then decipher the ingredients (it can be for a yummy punch that the class can have as a treat after the game). Each team must try to complete its mission before the other teams. As in a treasure hunt, each clue leads to an activity or a location with a task, which could be related to Israel or to learning Hebrew words, to get the next clue. All of the clues are English words but use Hebrew letters to spell them out—like a transliterated secret code.

Stop the Flood *(Type: Teaching; grades K-3)* This game expresses two ideas based on commentaries and midrash about the story of Noah and the ark. One is that God caused the flood as a do-over because boundaries—personal, physical, etc.—were being crossed and not respected, and such violations have consequences. The second idea is that Noah built the ark over a period of three hundred years to give the people time for self-improvement.

How to play: Have students build a city out of Legos in the bottom of a big tub or wading pool. Students then come up with situations where people cross boundaries and don't respect each other. For example, "My little brother uses my toys without asking," or, "Someone steals a candy bar from a store." For each example, the class decides how many cups of water will go in the tub, based on how serious they perceive the problem to be. The little brother using his sibling's toys without asking might rate one cup of water, while stealing a candy bar might rate three or four cups. Write all the scenarios with their water amounts on blank index cards. Shuffle the index cards, let students pick a card and read the problem, then add the appropriate amount of water to the pool. Note: Nonreaders can draw pictures of the problem on card stock, then use those drawings as the deck of cards. Or you can gather their ideas verbally, then out of class find images that match their problems and put them on cards.

As each cup of water gets added to the tub, it begins to flood the Lego city (which represents the world). However, if students can offer a solution to the problem, such as, "Instead of yelling at my little brother for taking my toy, I will remind him gently, and then let him play with it for a few minutes," they can take water out of the tub. There are many ways to adapt this game, such as adding a time limit, having the teacher add and subtract the water, or giving students a goal, to make it compatible with your class. Because of the messy nature of this game, playing outside or with a plastic drop cloth might be helpful.

Card Games

There are various styles of card games. Feed Your Wolves, described earlier, is one. Here are some others:

CHiP In—The Competing High Priorities Game *(Type: Teaching; grades 8-12)* In this game that I created, players explore the priorities at stake in complicated, real-life, moral situations and determine which priority should override the others. To play, each person picks five Value Chips (such as Family, Popularity, Wealth, Education, Respect, etc. There are eighteen different types of chips). Each round, a different player acts as the judge (as in Apples to Apples) and reads a Situation Card out loud from the deck. Each player then puts in his or her top-priority Value Chip for the given situation. Starting with the player to the left of the judge, each player defends his or her chip, explaining why that priority is most important. The judge decides which argument is the most compelling and awards the card to that player. Then the next player gets to be the judge. After everyone has had the opportunity to be judge twice, whoever has the most cards wins. Use this game as a means for exploring, expressing, and debating Jewish values.

Jewish Values Challenge Cards *(Type: Teaching; grades 6-12)* Created by Robyn Faintich, this deck contains thirty-two different cards through which students explore real-life challenges that can be handled using Jewish approaches. There are many different ways to use this deck.

You can also easily create your own card game with card stock, or, if you're more ambitious, create custom cards through a printer. (See behrmanhouse.com/jec for additional resources.)

Game Shows

It's tempting to base a game show on an existing one, but it's more effective to create one based on the content of your lesson. There are, of course, exceptions, such as *Hebrew Hollywood Squares* or *What's My Line*, using people from *Tanach* or Jewish history. Here are some never-before-seen-on-TV (yet!) examples:

Benefit of the Doubt *(Type: Review; all ages)* After a lesson on the mitzvah of giving others the benefit of the doubt, call up three "audience" members to be the players, and have the rest of the group judge their answers. Describe a situation in which a person seems like he or she might be doing something not so great. Each contestant has to find a way to give the person in the situation the benefit of the doubt. For each round, the group decides which player had the best alternate way of looking at the situation, and that player receives a point.

What Would Aaron Do? *(Type: Review; grades 4-8)* This show has two contestants and a few students chosen ahead of time as the actors. The rest of the group is the audience. Play this game after completing a unit on Aaron, Moses's brother, focusing, among other things, on his unique leadership qualities as a pursuer of peace. In this game, the student actors perform scenes that have some conflict, such as two good friends arguing. The actors freeze at some point at the height of the conflict, and the host (the educator) leads the audience in shouting, "What would Aaron do?" The contestant who hits the buzzer first gets a chance to act the part of Aaron and describe how to fix the problem. If the audience agrees with the contestant, that contestant gets a point. If not, the other player suggests a way to fix the problem.

• • •

There are very few Jewish-related subjects that can't be made into games, either by the teacher presenting the material or the students reflecting on what they have learned. Games can also be used in Project Based Learning (see chapter 9) and are perfect for family education (see chapter 12). Using creative games in the classroom that truly promote critical-thinking skills will create lasting memories for students—and are a sophisticated tool for helping them grow.

Ready to plan your game or help your students plan theirs? Use the game design template and begin!

Game Design Plan

NAME OF GAME:

PREPARATION FOR CREATION

1. Big theme or idea players will explore or understand:

2. Skill and knowledge objectives:

3. **Game format** – What format best suits your objectives? Possible ideas:

_____Board game   _____Physical game   _____Game show

_____Simulation game   _____Card game

CREATING THE GAME

4. **Game elements** – What element(s) will you use to convey your idea?
    Each element should clearly reflect your idea.

    _____Board   _____Video   _____Dice   _____

    _____Cards   _____Ball   _____Spinner   _____

5. **Game pieces** – If you use tokens or other pieces, how will they reflect your idea?

6. **Game objective** – clearly related to your lesson, theme, big idea, or learning objectives:

7. **Number of players:**

8. **Game rules** - How play proceeds:

    How play ends:

9. **Supplies needed:**

Creating Lasting Connections to Sacred Writings ▶ **3**

Text Activators

Whenever I ask adults, whether fellow educators or not, about their most memorable learning experience, the majority describe some activity that helped them understand the lesson. I've never heard, "That time I read the textbook and did some work sheets." Most people have powerful memories of teachers who made a huge impact because of their passion, humor, creativity, or kinesthetic lesson, which involved active learning. The lessons came to life with relevancy and sparked discussion and understanding.

What secrets can we learn from these experiences that we can apply to all our teaching, even—or especially—with the seemingly challenging learning of texts? Text Activators is a methodology that uses meaningful activities to connect learners to the essence of a text.

⬢ A Little Educational Philosophy

I hear and I forget
I see and I remember
I do and I understand.
　　　—ancient Chinese proverb

The best way to acquire a skill is to actually try and perform the action. This sounds obvious. If I want to learn to swim, for instance, I can watch a YouTube video with step-by-step instructions and even read a biography of Mark Spitz, but that doesn't mean I can really swim or even that I understand swimming. It is not until I get in the pool and try it for myself that I can truly understand what it means to come up for air, or what it feels like to paddle through water or try to stay afloat. When we learn new skills—riding a bike, reading, driving a car, typing (in the pre-texting days)—usually someone demonstrates it for us, and then we try it. The learning is in the doing, and the results last a lifetime.

But what happens when we want to acquire higher-order and critical-thinking skills that take practice and development? And what if these skills are to be used when studying text, with the goal of reaching a deeper and richer personal understanding?

If we want our students to learn by doing, then teaching Jewish texts—the lens by which we explore, reflect, discuss, relate to, and eventually own important concepts and big ideas (see Part 2)—presents interesting opportunities. Active learning can help students make sense of complex Jewish text. Additionally, understanding the importance of studying Jewish texts is itself a worthwhile goal, which can only be discovered through the act of digging deep into the text and its layers of meaning.

"Learning is not a spectator sport," according to noted educator Arthur W. Chickering. "Students do not learn much just by sitting in class listening to teachers, memorizing pre-packaged assignments, and spitting out answers. They must talk about what they are learning, write about it, relate it to past experiences, apply it to their daily lives. They must make what they learn part of themselves."[1] That's our ultimate goal as Jewish educators: to help our students make their learning part of themselves.

⬡ Practical Tools

The key to successfully connecting students to text, whether it's *Tanach* or Talmud, is engaging them in the ideas, the ongoing discussions, and the deeper meanings as they relate to them individually. When we give students meaningful activities—Text Activators—to explore the ideas and discover their personal relevancy, students feel like valued participants in the ongoing, centuries-old process of studying sacred writings.

To create Text Activators, we first have to determine the big idea, lesson, or goal for the piece of text we are learning with our students. Then we need to develop an activity that helps students understand the concept as a general construct, a metaphor, a personal experience, or a springboard for discussion.

Text Activators work well as set inductions before examining the actual text and can also be used throughout a lesson. The "active" part of Text Activators is important—physical movement and the use of senses.

Let's look at some Text Activators in action.

TEXT ACTIVATOR 1 · *Grades 4-8*

Text: In Genesis (chapter 27), Isaac gives Jacob the blessing meant for Esau. Isaac is said to be blind, so his wife, Rebecca, who believes Jacob to be more deserving, helps Jacob fool his father by dressing him in animal skins to simulate the hairy arms of Esau.

Understanding or Goal: Generate discussion about whether Isaac knew he was really giving the blessing to Jacob, and if so, what might that mean?

Text Activator: After reading the text, have students break into groups of three. Give one blindfold to each group. The students will take turns wearing the blindfold for each of three rounds.

First round: First person must identify others in group just by touching their arms.

Second round: Second person must identify others just by touching their shoes.

Third round: Third person must identify others just by hearing their voices.

Gather the whole class back together, and pick one volunteer to be blindfolded while people try to disguise their voices and see if the blindfolded volunteer can guess everyone's identity.

Then discuss: Could Isaac have known it was Jacob all along, and if so, what might that mean? What can we learn from this in our own lives? Have we ever allowed ourselves to be deceived for our own good? For the good of others?

TEXT ACTIVATOR 2 · *Grades 5-12*

Text: In Exodus (chapter 2), the "new Pharaoh" rises up and enslaves the Hebrews, but no names are mentioned until Moses is born.

Understanding or Goal: Names are more than just a way to identify us. Our names tell us about ourselves. The lack of names in this section reflects the slave status of the Hebrews. Not until the potentiality of freedom comes into play—with the birth of Moses—do we read names again.

Text Activator: This can be used as a set induction activity or right after reading the passage. Each student gets a "Hello, My Name Is" tag.

A quarter of the students get their own names.

A quarter of the students get tags with made-up names (not anybody else in the class).

Half the students get tags with nothing on them.

Inform students that for the rest of the session they must wear their name tags and refer to each other, as will you, only by the name on the tag. If there is nothing on the tag, then you can decide how to refer to them—"you there," "hey you," "what's your name," or something like that. Or just ignore them, since they don't have a name. Have students get up, move around, and talk to each other. Then carry on the lesson as long as you need for them to get the idea.

NOTE

There are many ways to understand and teach Jewish text, and even if you don't agree with the goal of this example, it serves to illustrate how the concept works and hopefully will inspire your own ideas.

3

Process afterward: How did each group feel? Was it hard to be arbitrarily given a name (this happened to slaves in America). Did it feel good to have your own name? Did it make you feel somewhat superior? What did you think about the people with no names? How did it feel not to have a name?

Then discuss: Have there been times in your lives that you have felt "nameless?" What does it mean to be nameless?

TEXT ACTIVATOR 3 · *Grades 6 and up*

Text: In Numbers, God gives the Land of Israel to the Israelites, who insist on sending twelve scouts (spies) ahead to see it first. Ten return with negative reports, while two of the scouts give positive assessments. Focus on Numbers 13:30-33, particularly the bolded phrase:

> And Caleb stilled the people before Moses and said: "We should go up at once and possess it, for we shall surely overcome it." But the men who had gone up with him said: "We are not able to go up against the people, for they are stronger than we." And they spread an evil report of the land that they had spied out unto the children of Israel, saying: "The land through which we have passed to spy it out is a land that eats up the inhabitants thereof; and all the people that we saw in it are men of great stature. and there we saw the Nephilim, the sons of Anak, who come of the Nephilim; and **we were like grasshoppers in our own eyes, and so we were in theirs.**"

Understanding or Goal: The way we think about ourselves is reflected in the image we project about ourselves, consciously or not, which in turn affects the way others see and treat us.

Text Activator: From a deck of cards, pull out some royalty cards (kings, queens, and jacks) and some aces, twos, and threes. You will not need the rest of the deck. Make sure that there are enough cards so that if you give each student one card, some would get the royalty cards, but more would get the lower cards. Then give each student a card face down. They cannot look at it. When you say, "Cards up," each person holds the card face up on their foreheads so everyone else can see, but they themselves cannot see their own card. Then you say, "Mingle," and everyone interacts for a few minutes, treating each other according to the card showing on their foreheads: Face cards are treated like royalty, and low cards are treated lowly (like grasshoppers). For example, people might want to steer clear of the lowly people or hang out with royalty. They should be encouraged to speak to each other but to make sure not to use words that would let the other person know what his or her card is. No "Your Highness," no "King," no "Queen," etc. Have all students return to their seats and put their cards face down, still not looking at them.

Then discuss: What card did you think you were? Why? How did it feel to be that card? How did others treat you? What image were you projecting? This activity can be done either before or after studying the text.

TEXT ACTIVATOR 4 · *Grades 4-12*

Text: Book of Esther, chapters 1-2.

Understanding or Goal: The seeds are planted for the Jews' salvation. God is working behind the scenes, even when we do not realize it (in our own lives, too).

Text Activator: For this activity, you will need a variety of seed packets with different flower or vegetable seeds. Take half the packets and empty each into a little baggie or other non-labeled package. The seeds in the original packets will be used in the first half of the activity, and the unidentifiable seeds will be used for the second half.

Students can work in pairs. Hand each pair a seed packet in its original packaging. Ask them to look at it, observe it, then answer the following questions:

- List all the ways you know what the seeds will grow.
- How can you be certain that the seeds in the packet will really grow what you think they will?
- Do you like the seeds you were given?
- What must you do to make sure the seeds actually grow?

After students have discussed (or written down) the answers with their partner, have a few share their answers with the class.

Then hand out the mystery seed packets. Have them look at them carefully and try to figure out what the seeds are meant to grow. Then ask:

- How do you know what this packet will grow?
- How do you feel about that?
- Would you plant them anyway? Why or why not.
- If you knew that God picked these seeds just for you, would you be more or less likely to plant them to see what comes up? Why?

Scaffold: If God gave you seeds that would potentially help you in the future, what would they be for?

Then: As you go through the text of the first two chapters of the book of Esther, have students point out all of the "seeds" that God "plants" that will end up saving the Jews later in the story.

TEXT ACTIVATOR 5 · *Grades 7-12*

Text: In Numbers (chapter 16), Korah leads a rebellion against Moses and Aaron, challenging their leadership by saying, "The entire congregation is holy, and God is in their midst. So why do you raise yourselves above God's assembly?"

Understanding or Goal: We *are* all holy, and even though we can't all be leaders, we each have important roles to play throughout the day and throughout our lives.

Text Activator: Break students into groups of five to seven people, and give each an envelope with their secret assignment in it. All the envelopes actually contain the same instructions:

You must put together a skit about what you have learned so far in class (from the beginning of the year). Everyone has to have <u>exactly</u> the same size part, and no one can be the director or take charge. Everyone must participate equally. You have ten minutes to put this together.

Feel free to circulate while students attempt this. Make sure that no one takes a leadership role. At the end of ten minutes, chances are they will have nothing to show for it—except frustration.

Then discuss the challenges they might have had and why. In life, we also have roles. What are some of the roles we take on every day (e.g., son/daughter/sibling/student/class clown/jock/tech expert)? Are leaders necessary? Why or why not?

TEXT ACTIVATOR 6 · *Grades 3-12*

Text: In *Pirkei Avot* (1:14), Hillel says:

If I am not for myself, who will be for me?
And if I am only for myself, what am I?
And if not now, when?

Understanding or Goal: We have to take care of ourselves, and we have an obligation to help others. We shouldn't put off helping either ourselves or others.

Text Activator: Break students into three groups. Assign one line of the text to each group, and give groups fifteen to twenty minutes to come up with three different scenarios that explore ways to understand their line. They will be making a tableau for each scenario. For example, for the first line—"If I am not for myself, who will be for me?"—the tableau could be sticking up for oneself against a bully. Another tableau might depict expressing one's authentic self regardless of what others might think, and so on.

As each group performs its three tableaux, have students from other groups explain what they are seeing. Is that what the originators of the tableaux had in mind? Are there other ways to interpret the line? Then see what the commentators say, too.

TEXT ACTIVATOR 7 · *Grades 5-12*

Text: Book of Proverbs

Understanding or Goal: Ancient texts can provide relevant, important wisdom and tools we can use in guiding our lives.

Text Activator: Students will create their own Text Activators by holding a "Proverbs Fair." After an initial introduction to the book of Proverbs, have students work on their own or in pairs and pick from a "Bag O' Proverbs" a particular proverb by chapter and verse. Teach them how to look up the proverb in the *Tanach* (a good skill to learn) and have them read what it says.

Steps:

1. Students try to figure out the meaning of the proverb on their own and write it down (see work sheet at www.behrmanhouse.com/jec).

2. Students ask others—parents, teachers, etc.—what they think it might mean and write it down.

3. Students look up various commentaries (there are many books of commentaries, as well as online sources) and write down what some of the commentators say. Students then think of ways this proverb might apply in their lives.

4. Students create a booth (like at a science fair) that physically expresses the essence of their verse, combining many of the understandings—theirs, the adults they interviewed, and the commentators.

For example, students using Proverbs 10:11—"The mouth of the *tzadik* [righteous one] is a wellspring of life, but the mouth of the *r'sha'im* [wicked ones] conceals [their] harm"—might design a booth with two giant mouths, one labeled *tzadik* and the other labeled *rasha*, with holes in them. Out of each mouth, students throw pieces of paper to the observers. The papers from the *tzadik*'s mouth contain important life lessons and guidance, while the pieces of paper coming from the *rasha*'s mouth would contain thinly disguised mean messages.

As observers visit each booth, students explain their proverb and engage the observers with it. Students also share how this proverb is relevant in their lives, and ask observers to see if they can apply it to their own lives.

Here is another example, from Proverbs 11:14: "When there are no strategic plans a nation will fall [to the enemy], but in much counsel there is victory." Students focus on more personal understandings: the best plan derives from hearing many opinions during a planning process; or, one must think through all the possible alternatives for action in order to choose the best course.

Students plan an activity for their observers using two Jenga towers. When a student says "Go!" the observers, working in groups of three or four, pull out three pieces at a time from the first Jenga tower. They have no time to think, just pull out the first three pieces they can. Chances are the tower will fall pretty quickly. Then, students give the observers at least one minute to discuss options and strategies for the second Jenga tower. Students encourage observers to consider all the angles and really listen to each other's ideas before carefully pulling out three pieces. Chances are that the tower will not fall. Then the observers can relate the Jenga exercise to their understandings of the verse and, of course, discuss personal applications.

TEXT ACTIVATOR 8 · *Grades K-12*

This activity (and its variations) isn't about a specific text but rather explores the process of learning Jewish texts or exegesis.

Understanding or Goal:
- There are many layers of meaning in a Jewish text, and we can learn something valuable from each layer.
- There is a methodology to learning text that has spanned the generations; by understanding and engaging with this Jewish method of interpretation, we continue that tradition.
- The goal is to experience what it means to go deeper into learning something.

Text Activator: Going into the Garden!

The Hebrew word *pardes* means "orchard" or "garden." The Hebrew acronym *PaRDeS*, refers to four levels of depth in learning Jewish text. The connection between these two words isn't just coincidental. After all, the Torah is known as the Tree of Life. Just as there are many ways to try to understand trees—up close, examining the bark, leaves, and fruit; or from a distance, taking in the whole tree and its surroundings—there are many ways to understand our sacred texts. The following activities exemplify the concept of different levels of text study.

RESOURCE

Here is a chart to give students. Review all the terms before engaging in a "Going into the Garden!" activity.

Letter	Meaning	
פ (p)	פְּשָׁט	*P'shat* – Simple, literal
ר (r)	רֶמֶז	*Remez* – Hint, suggestion
ד (d)	דְּרָשׁ	*D'rash* – Insight
ס (s)	סוֹד	*Sod* – Mystery, secret

Idea 1: If possible, take your students to visit a nearby orchard, botanical garden, or wooded area. Or you can visit a backyard, a nearby park, or even create an "orchard" out of chairs or other furniture. Then do one of the following:

- **Grades K-3:** Before the activity begins, lightly attach pictures of a puzzle box to the outer circle of trees. Attach puzzle pieces to the trees further in. After they gather the pieces, they can create the puzzle. This will help younger children understand that the puzzle pieces themselves make the puzzle, not just the pretty box.

- **Grades 4 and up:** Before the activity begins, put clues to solving a riddle, logic question, or complicated story (told from different angles) on different trees or in different areas of a garden. In the outermost ring of trees or plants, attach the same clue/puzzle pieces to every tree or group of flowers. Just like the *p'shat* of a text, it's a beginning, but it doesn't tell the whole story.

    As the students go deeper into the setting, they will discover more clues or puzzle pieces, representing the way we delve deeper into a text to learn more or to help us "put the pieces together." To complete the analogy, students will complete the puzzle, or the last clues or puzzle pieces will reveal a mystery or secret—the answer to the riddle, logic question, or story.

Scaffold for older students: Have them do this activity as a treasure hunt, in which the clues are verses of a text you are studying. Students have to discuss and figure out the meaning of each verse, which will lead them to the next clue.

When students first arrive at the park, have them write down or discuss what they see—what do they know about trees, the fruits (or whatever is grown), the park as a whole—from this vantage point? As you move deeper in, toward the center of the park, ask them to write about or discuss the same questions: What do they know about trees or the orchard from this vantage point? Ask them to find a tree, stand about six feet away from it, and describe the tree in as much detail as possible. Then ask them to repeat the process at three feet and then at mere inches away. They should describe exactly what they see and what they can tell you about trees in general, and this park in particular, from this vantage point. Find a place to sit and share students' descriptions. Ask how this might relate to learning a text. If it is possible to bring with you the text you are starting and do some learning in the orchard or garden, all the better!

Idea 2: Bring in images of a garden or orchard taken from different perspectives, along with photos of trees or flowers from various distances (including extreme close-ups). Alternatively, have students find images using their phones or computers, or take pictures and bring in the images. Then have a similar discussion to the one in the activity above. What can we know about trees or flowers in general from each of these images? What can we know about a specific tree or flower from these images? Do any of the images provide a complete understanding of the trees or flowers? Then you can relate it to learning text and teach about each level of *PaRDeS*.

Scaffold: Ask students to select four images, each visually representing one part of *PaRDeS*. For example, a super close-up of a tree or flower (maybe even with a bee pollinating it) would represent *Sod*—the "Secrets." Have students put the four images they choose on index cards and label them with the corresponding level. They can then use these throughout the learning. For example, perhaps they have an idea or insight to share. Which card might they hold up to represent that level? When reading Rashi or another commentary, which image might represent that comment?

• • •

Now it is your turn: Use the template on the next page to create your own Text Activators. First, choose one understanding or goal you want students to internalize, think about, discuss, or apply to the text (as seen in the above examples). Then, like the thesis of a paper, continually ask yourself, as you plan your Text Activator, if it truly serves the chosen understanding or goal. Just as with the games in chapter 2,

NOTE

Once students have participated in a *PaRDeS* activity, you can continue to reference these layers of learning as you use any Text Activator above, or one of your own creation. After a Text Activator, ask students how far "into the garden" this activity might have reached.

brainstorming with colleagues can be very helpful. Will this be used to introduce a lesson before students read the text, or will it be something they do after the first reading of the text?

Sometimes you can easily repurpose an activity for a secular lesson into a Text Activator. Years ago, I came across an activity to help public-school students with self-esteem issues and changed it to use for the verses about the spies. I've also adapted that same activity for use in an English lesson on *The Scarlet Letter*.

You will notice that in general, Text Activators are meant to lead to discussions, which usually foster interesting insights. With planning and imagination, your Text Activators will help students find personal relevancy and spark critical thinking.

Text Activator Planner

TEXT:

UNDERSTANDING OR GOAL?

Is it a set induction or study piece?

TEXT ACTIVATOR:

- -

TEXT:

UNDERSTANDING OR GOAL?

Is it a set induction or study piece?

TEXT ACTIVATOR:

PART TWO

Engaging with Jewish STEM—Spirituality, Theology, Ethics, and Maggid

I had never understood the lure of Sudoku. I admit I'm not really a "math person," but even so, many non-math folks seemed hopelessly hooked. I would look at it and think, "I don't even understand this." Then one day I visited my father, who uses puzzles as a way to keep his mind nimble, and he asked me if I knew the secrets of solving Sudoku. There were secrets to solving Sudoku? I asked him to show me, and not just to humor him; I was genuinely curious. Sure enough, he showed me a few tricks, had me practice, and suddenly I saw Sudoku in a whole new light. Afterward, I couldn't wait to try again and again.

What does this have to do with Jewish education? For a variety of reasons, our students sometimes resist their religious education. Perhaps it's because they don't know the secrets yet—the tricks, if you will, that make Judaism relevant and interesting—ways to see Judaism in a whole new light, things they might want to try again and again. The secret is integrating Jewish STEM.

One of the biggest trends in the secular educational world is the emphasis on STEM (science, technology, engineering, and math), which will hopefully better prepare our students, in a holistic way, for twenty-first-century professions and jobs, most of which don't even exist yet. In the Jewish educational world, we are trying to prepare our students for the future in a different, but equally important, way—perhaps even a more important way. So, what tools can we give students for success? What is the STEM equivalent in Judaism that will prepare our students for their future?

When we integrate **S**pirituality, **T**heology, **E**thics, and *Maggid* (storytelling) into everything we teach in a holistic way, we get our very own, very important Jewish STEM benefits. Why these four? The next chapters will explore how each of these areas is crucial to helping our students connect to their Judaism and how you can add them to your curriculum.

Spirituality
Tackling T'filah

▶ **4**

I once attended a large Shabbat dinner with a group of Jewish educators and rabbinical students. By way of connecting us all, the host asked the group a question: "What was your most meaningful prayer experience?" As people took turns answering, I noticed that most didn't pick a time or place in a traditional synagogue setting. Many answers involved nature locales—beaches, mountains, and, of course, Jewish summer camps. Other answers included places as diverse as the Western Wall, the ruins of a concentration camp, and a parent's hospital room. Moved and inspired, I tried to come up with my own best experience from a wonderful assortment of powerful options I felt blessed to choose from. Then I heard a rabbinical student answer the question in a really interesting way. "Instead of just asking myself what my most meaningful prayer experience was, I also want to know what God thinks, so to speak, my most meaningful experience was." I could hear the collective "Aha" in the room as everyone contemplated that. This student reminded us that ultimately t'filah is about creating and participating in a relationship with the Divine.

If you ask Jewish educators to name the most challenging topic to teach, many might say *t'filah*. It really isn't about the mechanics of prayers—teaching the words or tunes. That's the easy part. More difficult is helping students find meaning in the prayers. How do students relate to the ancient language and imagery of the siddur? If they don't understand the words, it can seem like gibberish. They often aren't exposed to models of adults engaged in passionate or meaningful *t'filah*, so they don't see the value in it. Summer camp seems to be an exception, a place where campers not only participate, but also lead and feel ownership of their *t'filah* experience. When I attended summer camp, we all enjoyed dressing in white and participating in Kabbalat Shabbat services. All the prayers before and after the meal felt meaningful because we did them as a community. How do we bring this visceral understanding into *t'filah* and rituals in non-camp settings? That is the big question.

We know that in Temple times, instead of structured prayer, Jews brought *korbanot* to the Temple, which we translate as "sacrifices." But the root of the word actually means to "draw near" or "show friendship." This ritual directly connected people to God in a way we can't really understand today. To aid students in finding that relationship, connection, and meaning in modern times, it's helpful to explore what God is (for more on ways to do this, see chapter 5) and how to engage with God through both communal and personal prayer.

◆ A Little Educational Philosophy

We in the Jewish educational world are already tuned into what *The Handbook of Spiritual Development in Childhood and Adolescence* claims:

> *In adolescence, spirituality is significant for the healthy, positive development of a person's sense of self—his or her identity—and for enabling identity to frame the individual's pursuit of a life path eventuating in idealized adulthood.*[1]

As Jewish educators, we believe in giving our students a strong spiritual foothold, but there is so much to teach and only so much time to do so. We want our students to love Judaism. But why? What is it about being Jewish that is important to us? After we answer that ourselves, then how do we instill a love of Judaism and, more importantly, help our students answer "Why be Jewish?" for themselves? If we can introduce concepts and ideas that will guide them on their life paths, we will have accomplished a lot. Giving students an understanding of why we pray, and inspiring their passion toward *t'filah* is a good start.

◆ Practical Tools

Before exploring ways to teach *t'filah*, we first have to figure out our goals. Teachers often say they strive for two overarching goals: fluency and personal connection. Each institution, however, must decide for itself which goals are most important for its purposes. Educator Hannah Dreyfus notes in her essay "Teaching Prayer: Obstacles, Goals, and Strategies" that there is a lot riding on this answer and looks to a synthesis of both fluency and personal connection.

> *[In a balanced educational prayer model, both] the fastidious formulation and presentation of language, as well as an understanding of one's actions are highlighted. Precise annunciation substantiates comprehension and focus. A comprehensive knowledge of the prayers facilitates the mind-blowing realization of what prayer truly is: The unique opportunity to stand before the Creator of the Universe. An ideal tefillah education would therefore synthesize these two goals—a fluency in the texts that weave together to form a dialogue, the fabric*

of man's most essential relationship.[2]

What are *t'filah*'s goals? Below are categories of fluency and personal connection broken into smaller, more specific goals. Your institution might have some *t'filah* goals that are not on this list, but the important point is, before trying to teach prayer, be clear about your educational goals. When undertaking the daunting task of teaching *t'filah*, figure out which goals are the most important both for the institutional objectives and for your overall curricula. If your ideas or goals conflict with your institution, a conversation with the head of your organization may be helpful to clarify the areas of compromise. Language usage, concepts of God, and other personal dynamics may differ not only between you and the institution, but also between you and your students. These all have to be negotiated with respect and openness from all parties. If we can view each discussion as a learning opportunity, the results will be more fruitful.

Let's look at possible *t'filah* goals, each of which is labeled with a letter that corresponds to examples on the following pages.

POSSIBLE T'FILAH GOALS

Students will:

A — Be able to follow along with all of the prayers, so they can participate in services.

B — Know prayers so they can feel comfortable in any Jewish place of worship.

C — Feel a connection to Jews all over the world because of their comfort with Jewish modes of worship that have similarities around the globe.

D — Understand the origins of the prayers and the structure of the services to gain an appreciation for and understanding of *t'filah*.

E — Delve deeply into the meanings of the prayers and find personal connections.

F — Explore the ways we relate to the infinite in a finite world.

G — Understand *t'filah* as a two-sided relationship with the Divine.

H — Use the traditional *t'filot* as a springboard for creating their own dynamic relationship with God through personal prayers.

I — Feel a connection with the idea of prayer, so that it will become a source of comfort in the future.

J — Gain a sense of community through the power of communal prayer.

K — Gain leadership opportunities.

L — Deepen their appreciation for the transformational potential of Jewish prayer.

M — Explore the idea that *t'filah* helps us partner with God in fixing and perfecting the world.

N — Acquire tools to have a transcendent experience with the Divine.

That's a lot of goals! Generally, it's best for educational programs or curricula to focus on just the ones they deem most important—which can change depending on grade level.

PUTTING GOALS INTO PRACTICE

Each of the following ideas corresponds to some of these *t'filah* goals. Target ages for the ideas are not included for a few reasons: You know your students and what they are capable of. You might be able to adjust or refine a particular idea to fit your needs. Or, it might spark another idea that is perfect for your class.

Photo Siddur
Goals: A–N

Students explore their personal relationship to each prayer through discovering who compiled or composed the prayer and why, as well as discussing the symbolic and poetic language with their peers. They then make creative connections to the *t'filah* using photography, artwork, and/or poetry (their own or others), in order to create a siddur that they can take ownership of, both literally and figuratively. Through this process, students reflect on the deeper, personal meaning of *t'filah*. To give them a different perspective, you can even have students switch *siddurim* with each other once in a while, and then discuss how a new siddur may or may not have affected their *t'filah* experience. (This full Project Based Learning unit is described in detail in chapter 9.)

Dancing with God: An Exploration of the Amidah
Goals: A, B, D, G, I, L, M, N

This multipart activity focuses on our interconnectedness with God and the choreography of the Amidah. Also, each of the parts can be used on its own. It is essential to use a relatable translation (no *thees* and *thous*) when doing this activity.

Part One

Pair up students—one "A" with one "B." Each student stays an A or B for each of the four rounds of this activity. Each round should last about five minutes.

First round: All A's introduce themselves to their B partners (pretending that they are meeting for the first time) and start a conversation.

Second round: All the A's are bosses, and all the B's are coming in for job interviews. Tell the B's to introduce themselves to their potential bosses and begin a conversation.

Third round: Each B is a King or a Queen. The A's have never met royalty before and are very excited—but also very nervous. Tell them to introduce themselves to the King or Queen and try to start a short conversation.

Fourth (and last) round: The A's are major movie stars or celebrities. The B's introduce themselves and try to start a conversation.

Afterward, ask students how each round was different. How did they each conduct themselves? Did anything change? Should it have? Did they stand differently? Move differently? When we "introduce ourselves" to God, would it be as friends, as meeting with the boss, with royalty, or with someone who seems beyond us? Could it be all of the above? When are the times we approach God in each of these ways?

Part Two

Play a clip from a period piece with a ballroom scene (many clips can be found from *Pride and Prejudice*, for example) that shows the formality and intricacy of a dance. Point out the initial bow and curtsy that begin the dance, and how each partner has to know all the steps. It is a true partnership. Unlike our current styles, these dances would look silly if someone did them by themselves.

Teach or review the movements we use for the Amidah—taking three steps back, three steps forward, then bowing. We can compare it to beginning a dance with God. Ask students to explain the similarities and also the differences. If we are dancing with God, then the Amidah is really about a partnership.

The dance must be a waltz, because everything is about three's. Show a video clip of a ballroom-competition waltz and ask students to note how the couple is moving, who is leading, etc. The count is in three's. What might three represent? Ask how the waltz might be a metaphor for our relationship with God. (See Part Four below for more about this.)

Part Three

When we are "introduced" to God in the Amidah, it says, "God of Abraham, God of Isaac, and God of Jacob." In many prayer books it also says, "God of Sarah, God of Rebecca, God of Rachel, and God of Leah." Any way you slice it, that's a lot of "Gods." Ask students why it doesn't just say "God of Abraham, Isaac, and Jacob," or "God of Sarah, Rebecca, Rachel, and Leah." Why does it differentiate between each person?

Have students draw a picture of themselves (a stick figure is fine, but ask them to add some details particular to themselves, such as a baseball if they like to play, or science equipment if that is their passion). Then have them list all the relationships they have. For example: child/parent, student/teacher, friends, cousins, grandchild/grandparent, performer/audience, teammates, player/coach. Then ask them to consider whether they act or relate the same way in every relationship. If not, why not? In what ways do they act or relate the same no matter what the relationship? How might God relate to us as individuals that is different from the way God relates to other people? In what ways might it be the same for all people? What might each of our forebears mentioned in the Amidah represent? What does it mean that each are referred to individually and not as a collective group?

Part Four

The dance begins! Go through the three sections of the Amidah and discuss them.

Section 1: Reacquaintance with God—in **Avot** (in some traditions known as

TIP

This is a great time to use EDpuzzle (Edpuzzle.com) or Playposit (Playposit.com), which are both interactive platforms for engaging students with questions while they watch a video on their own devices. (See chapter 10 for more information on how to use both programs.)

4

NOTE

While some of this activity centers on the daily Amidah, you can also adapt it for the Shabbat Amidah by focusing on the sections that appear in both.

Avot V'imahot, Patriarchs and Matriarchs) we remind ourselves before whom we stand and consider the idea of personal protection. What does that mean to us? In **G'vurot** (God's Might), we see that situations that feel hopeless can be turned around. Do we ever feel that way in our own lives? Go through the list of God's acts in G'vurot—supporting the fallen, healing the sick, releasing the captive, etc.—and ask for examples of what students have seen (or haven't seen) in their lives. In the **K'dushah**, which is recited only in the presence of a minyan, we rise up on our toes three different times.

Section 2: This section—***K'dushat Hashem*** (You Are Holy) through ***Sh'ma Kolainu*** (Hear Our Voice)—begins the real dance and examines how we should emulate God. How can we be partners with God? When does God dance solo, and when do we dance together? Have students go through each part of this section with a partner and explore these questions. For example, in *R'fu'ah*, we ask God to heal us. How do we partner with God on this? Certainly doctors, nurses, and EMTs do this. But what other ways can we help? For example, how do we aid somebody in emotional pain? You might ask each pair of students to explore just one blessing and present their ideas to the rest of the group, leading the group in discussion. Alternatively, the pair can create a drawing or present a skit showing how they can partner with God and then present to the group.

Section 3: This section—***Modim*** (beginning with "We gratefully thank you")—gives thanks for presenting a model for us to emulate and also acknowledges what is beyond us. We are grateful to a dance partner who teaches us to be a better dancer. In this way, we thank God for being our partner and also our teacher. Students can think about and share the things they are grateful for. Are they similar to what is in the Amidah? Which lines in this section can we relate to?

We end the Amidah—finishing our dance—by bowing, taking three steps back, bowing left, right, and center, and taking three steps forward.

Moving Prayers
Goals: A, B, E, H, I, J, K

Have student pairs take any prayer they are learning and try to create representational hand movements or gestures for each phrase or line (using the English translation, as needed). Have students think carefully about gestures that might express the essence of the line—they shouldn't just be unconnected or random movements. When pairs have completed their Moving Prayer, they should practice it and then present it to the whole group while reciting or singing the prayer in Hebrew. If using this activity with older learners, they can discuss which movements might have given them a different insight into the prayer. Alternatively, each pair can come up with just a section and then teach it to the whole group. When all the groups have completed the prayer, they will have created the movements for it together as a class. This is a way for students to connect with prayer on a kinesthetic level.

Prayer Poetry Slam Service

Goals: D, E, F, H, K, L, N

Each student takes a prayer and finds a quiet place to study it in depth. What is the prayer trying to say? What parts contain poetic imagery? What does the imagery mean? When was the prayer written and by whom? (This part can be researched.) Then, have the students write poems that express in their own words what the prayer is all about. Afterward, hold a Prayer Poetry Slam Service. Either students can read their poems during the regular service, after each prayer, or the whole service consists of just the poems (depending on the congregational outlook).

The next two t'filah activities are adapted from an experiential learning curriculum that was created for the South African Board of Jewish Education.[3]

The Power of Communal Prayer

Goals: I, J, L, M

Initiate a discussion encouraging participants to express their wishes for the world: an end to poverty, hunger, crime, racism, anti-Semitism; a wish for peace in Israel, in the world. Have them state their wish in a single sentence and take turns saying their sentences out loud. Then, have all the students yell their sentences as loud as they can all at once.

Next, have them come to a consensus about one thing they all want. They can debate if necessary. Once they are all in agreement, turn that communal desire into a one-liner. For example: Peace in Israel! No more crime! Heal the sick! Go around the group and ask each person to shout that line aloud—as loud as possible. Then have the group say it aloud in unison three times.

Finally, have each student close his or her eyes and spend fifteen seconds visualizing what the world or their lives would be like if this problem were fixed. Then, on your command, give a three-second countdown, at the end of which all the kids will begin chanting the one-liner in a hushed voice. Slowly begin to raise the volume until you are all shouting your lungs out!

Lead a discussion afterward. Here are some questions to ask:
- How did it feel when you shouted out what you wanted by yourself? When you each shouted out your individual desires?
- Was it hard to agree on one thing?
- How did it feel to shout the new desire by yourself? With everyone?
- How did the meaning of your chanting change after you visualized the world with that change?
- Do our words have power?
- What happens if the slogan that people yell out is negative?
- What is a minyan? Why do we pray in a minyan?

NOTE

As a passionate Jewish educator, it's hard to hear students say, "Services are super boring," or "I don't believe in God." Help students dig deeper without judgment, allowing them to explore how to overcome these challenges. Sharing our own challenges and struggles will help students understand that it is natural to feel them. Brent Davidoff, who helped create the curriculum for the South African Board of Jewish Education, has a powerful suggestion for teachers:

It is essential that we fuse our own personal religious experiences. The way you relate to God, the way you communicate with God, what you find difficult and what brings you joy are some examples of the things we have traditionally been told to avoid expressing when teaching. But, can we honestly expect learners to form and inform their relationship with God without us having shown them that we too have been through a process of exploration and discovery? It is not your conclusions, however, that are necessarily being shared but rather the universal experience of searching: searching for answers, searching for meaning.

4

- What are the advantages? Disadvantages?

Here are some potential discussion touchstones:
- Judaism is a religion of community, of people coming together and helping each other in all aspects of life. We can see this clearly through prayer: how we come together as a community to pray, and how our prayers are written in the plural form to include everyone.
- Many people believe that our prayers become more potent and powerful when we pray together, and that when we pray together, we actually do have the ability to change this world for the better.
- Praying is more than saying words out loud together. It is about thinking together, feeling together. Imagine the effect we can have on the world when we all think the same good thoughts together.
- Now imagine we are communally thinking and saying negative things about this world and other people. This has a potent but detrimental effect on us and the world.

Conclusion: Go through the siddur and examine prayers like Ashrei and Aleinu, which make use of the plural form of Hebrew. Solicit thoughts and ideas.

Or try saying the Sh'ma together aloud. Reflect on what it means and how it feels to say it together.

Making Prayer Personal

Goals: D, E, G, H, I, M

The *Anshei Knesset Hagedolah* (the Great Assembly), which began to compile the prayer book in the middle of the third century BCE, and others who followed had the needs of the entire Jewish people in mind, including future generations. We need to see their words through our own eyes. When we achieve this, prayer can become a personalized, meaningful, and perhaps enjoyable experience.

Before the exercise below, ask: What are some of the challenges of the prayer service? Why might these be challenges? What are potential benefits of the prayer service? Share your own answers with the group.

Begin by asking students to choose a prayer from any part of the prayer service, taking a section that they don't easily understand. Have them find a quiet space either somewhere in the sanctuary or outdoors.

Then have students create a "Personal Prayer Cheat Sheet," doing some research and using the prompts below. Students should:
- Research and record some basic facts about the prayer: Who wrote it? When was it written? Why was it written? Does it have any special choreography or movements? Any denominational changes? If so, why did that denomination change it? Try to find different translations. Are some more easy to relate to? What is the overall tone or feeling of the different translations?
- Ask themselves, "What does this prayer ask for or express?" Record the answers on their Personal Cheat Sheet.
- Ask themselves, "How would such an idea benefit the world?" Then draw a picture or create a graphic depicting a before and after.

- Then ask themselves, "How would my life improve from such an idea?" Record answer.
- Rewrite the prayer in their own words. It can be prose or poetry.

Once students have completed their "Personal Prayer Cheat Sheets," each student should write a short speech "justifying" the request or idea expressed in his or her prayer. Students can take turns reading the original versions of their prayers, their own versions of the prayers, and their speeches. For each prayer, the whole group should try to come up with a one-line slogan or catchphrase, which students can add to their cheat sheets.

Quick Ideas

These ideas come from Senior Jewish Educator at Penn Hillel Rabbi Josh Bolton's list of *100 Prompts, Provocations and Situations for Jewish Growth on Campuses.*[4] His list was meant for college students, but middle and high school students can probably handle them as well.

- Read the morning prayer Elohai N'shamah. What does it mean when we say the soul God has given us is "pure"?
  Goals: E, L
- Hand out copies of Modeh/Modah Ani. Ask students to recite it upon waking each morning for one week. Come back together and discuss.
  Goals: E, H, L
- Read the Sh'ma in its entirety. Ask students: "How would you relate to the second paragraph if you were a Cambodian sustenance farmer? How would you relate to it if you were "ancient man?" How does it relate to you?
  Goals: E, F, M

Other Quick Ideas

- Add a meditation before beginning a prayer session.
- Let teachers hand out preprinted cards that say, "Please help me focus on my *t'filah,*" so they can join in services without having to police or "shush" students. Schools with non-Jewish teachers can ask those teachers to help quiet students so Jewish teachers can model focus in prayer.
- Take students to see how different denominations pray. Or ask people from other denominations to come and speak about what prayer means to them.
- Show students that prayer can happen almost anywhere and find different, interesting places to engage in *t'filah.*

CELEBRATING SUCCESS

A few years ago, the education team at Congregation Rodeph Sholom's religious school in New York City—Jay Rapoport, Tirza Arad, Kerith Braunfeld, and Marcia Stein—wanted to transform their student *t'filah* program to make it a more empowering, personal, and communal spiritual experience. Tirza Arad summed up the program this way: "Prayer is like a vehicle that transports us to a different place. We need to know how to drive it; we don't necessarily have to know how the engine works."

Their program includes a combination of visual *t'filah* (the *t'filot* and accompanying images, developed by Dan Medwin, are projected at the front of the room) and Experiential Learning activities which connect students to each prayer on a personal and communal level. The school year begins with a focus on creating an experience around a particular prayer each week—in essence, building a service week by week in a purposeful way. Sometimes photographs of past weeks' experiences are added to the visual *t'filah*, so that each time the prayer comes up, students can remember, reflect on, and reconnect to that experience as they go through that prayer. During *t'filah* each week, the educators make sure to include singing, movement, open-ended discussion questions, storytelling, and more. The students have indeed been transported.

• • •

As much as possible, students should lead *t'filah*, even if it is done together with an adult. If any student plays a musical instrument and can be encouraged to learn the tunes and play during *t'filah* (if appropriate), it would add much to the experience for all students.

With a commitment to exploring the different facets of *t'filah*, we hope to meet our educational goals while giving students the lifelong gift of prayer.

Theology ▶ 5
God and Other Big Ideas

Years ago, when I first started teaching Tanach to seventh graders, I was constantly blown away by their depth and spirituality. They very much wanted to connect to something divine, and they had big, important questions to ask. As a new teacher, I didn't realize that I was supposed to cover a lot of content and not let our discussions from their questions take over our class. Eventually, I understood that I needed to add those questions and ideas into the actual lessons, and, in fact, the students were completely involved in lessons that introduced or dealt with big ideas.

Many years later, when I was developing LaunchBox, a toolkit of materials to connect preteens and teens with their Judaism, I went into four very different student populations and interviewed more than 250 students. These children asked me big philosophical and theological questions, and admitted that such topics hadn't been covered in their religious educations. I realized that I, too, had never discussed these ideas or questions when I was in religious school (or in secular school for that matter). Only much later in life, when exposed to the richness and depth of Jewish thought, did I finally connect, which eventually changed my life.

One of the biggest challenges in Jewish education is helping our learners understand the relevance and importance of Judaism. With younger students, in particular, we have many successes in this area. And yet, so many students leave their Jewish studies after their *b'nei mitzvah*, just when they are starting to contemplate the bigger questions in life (What is God? What is the meaning of life? Fate or free will? Why is there evil? Is there an afterlife?). Many kids never get a chance to explore these bigger ideas through a Jewish lens. Even students who do continue their Jewish education don't always get to address these issues. As a result, they don't see the practical relevance of Judaism in their lives. Incorporating the big philosophical and theological ideas, even at the earliest stages of learning, and wrestling with important concepts and questions within a Jewish framework can help students more readily recognize the depth and breadth of Jewish thought and connect more powerfully.

⬢ A Little Educational Philosophy

What are Big Ideas, and how can incorporating them into our curricula help our students? Although often used interchangeably with Enduring Understandings (see Chapter 8), in this chapter the term Big Ideas refers to philosophical and theological issues, questions, and paradoxes we grapple with as Jews. Some of these—the meaning of life, good and evil, who am I—are reflected in general society and can be explored through a Jewish lens. Other Big Ideas are specific to Judaism, such as the oneness of God, responsibility to the Jewish People, and what chosen actually means. In all cases, the more exposure to and exploration of the Big Ideas in a Jewish educational context we give students, the more they will look to Judaism as a viable and sustaining part of their lives.

In *The Philosophy Gym: 25 Short Adventures in Thinking*, author Stephen Law encourages the teaching of Big Ideas because, "An advantage of a little philosophical training is that it can provide the skills needed to think independently and question what others might take for granted. It can also help fortify your courage in making a moral stand."[1] In a world full of contradictory messages, giving students a strong Jewish philosophical foundation to work from provides a powerful structure in challenging times.

Moreover, the richness of Jewish thought and theology manifests throughout the different movements of Judaism, so if we can expose our students to the entire palette of ideas from the various streams, we encourage them to make decisions about their Judaism.

⬢ Practical Tools

This section is divided into two parts. Part One deals with putting God in the curriculum, including activities for various age groups. Part Two focuses on creating other Big Ideas activities, with concrete examples from Jewish texts, themes and concepts.

GOD

Perhaps one of the biggest dilemmas in Jewish education is how to explain God. It makes sense. There are so many ways to understand the infinite—and we are finite, so none of them really do God justice. And then there are the names. Which to choose? God (loaded with so much imagery and weight, including the ever-present

Greco-Christian guy with a robe-and-long-white-beard image), Hashem (often colored by one's denominational lens), Lord, Adonai, Elohim, *Sh'chinah*, etc.? And how do we explain they are all one? How do we explain what "God is one" means, which is different from "There is one God?" Even writing this section is challenging because the minute we bring discussion of God into anything, it becomes sensitive. As Rabbi David Aaron, an author and founder of Isralight, writes, "Each one of us is like a drop in the ocean trying to comprehend the ocean."[2] I won't even get started on use of pronouns for the Divine.

In spite of the challenges of talking about God, or maybe because of them, it is imperative that we try. Here are four activities to introduce ideas about God. The most important thing is to get students questioning and discussing. Each activity is marked as "beginner," "intermediate," or "advanced." There are no suggested ages, however, because while some ten-year-olds are capable of very deep and complex thought, some seventeen-year-olds are not. You know your students and can best judge what they are ready for.

One God, Many Names

For beginner, intermediate, and advanced contemplation.

This activity includes many parts, and, of course, you can add more yourself. Scale it up or down, depending on how you scaffold it, which parts you choose, and which questions you ask.

See the following page for a list of many names we use for God, taken from different texts, including *Tanach*, the Talmud, and the siddur. (Consider translating the list into Hebrew for more fluent students.) Below are some ideas for its use:

- Have students go through the list quickly and check off the names they connect with, putting an "X" next to the names with which they don't connect. Then discuss.
- Go through each name as a class or assign a group of names to different pairs of students. Discuss what image each name conjures up for them.

  Scaffold: Have students pick the names that are most meaningful to them and write a prayer using one or more of those chosen names.
- Model different Lenses of Questioning (see chapter 1) by having students pick five names (or assign them) and answer the following Lens Questions for each name:

  Orange: Have you heard this name for God before? If so, where?

  Blue: What attribute of God might this name express?

  Green: In what kind of situation might you find yourself using this name?

  Yellow: What is the strength of the name?

  Gray: What is the weakness of the name?

  Red: How does this name make you feel?

  Scaffold: Students come up with different Lens Questions for some of the names, and then use them for discussion.
- Have students look through a siddur for familiar prayers. They may need your guidance to find them, or you might want to do this together as a

TIP

For younger students, keep it simple. Write a few categories of prayer—giving thanks, help in a hard situation, etc.—on a large sheet of paper and tape it to the wall. Have students help you place the names of prayers they already know in the right categories. Then take ten or so of the most common names of God and write them on index cards so that students can tape them to the paper in the categories in which they feel they belong.

class. While they are looking, ask, "What are all the different kinds of prayers?" On a giant Post-it Note, have students list the various forms of prayer and reasons people pray, with two columns for each example, one for the personal level and one for the macro level. For example, people might pray for strength in different situations—I need strength to get through a personal challenge, and we (the Jewish people, our community, our country, humanity in general) need strength to get through a crisis or tough time on a macro level. For each moniker on the list of God's names, have students answer, "What kind of prayers or in what context might this name be helpful for us to use? Which attributes of God does each name conjure up? And which attribute of God would be helpful in which prayer situations?"

Have students write the names from the list on Post-it Notes and put them next to the appropriate kind of prayer. For example, "Rock of Israel" might go next to "prayers asking for strength for the Jewish people as a whole"; "Ruler of the Universe" might go next to "giving thanks."

Scaffold: Ask students: Is there a name you'd like to add to this list? What attribute does it convey? Why would this be a worthy addition?

At any time during these activities, ask: If we say "God is One," why are there so many names for God?

The Many Names of God

___ God	___ Shalom
___ Lord	___ Shepherd
___ The Name	___ Rock of Israel
___ Merciful One	___ Healer of the Sick
___ Eternal One	___ Freer of the Captives
___ Dweller	___ Clother of the Naked
___ Strong One	___ Opener of Blind Eyes
___ Master of the World	___ Supporter of the Fallen
___ The Most High	___ Straightener of the Bent
___ Our Father	___ Fashioner of Light
___ Our King	___ Maker of Peace
___ The Creator	___ Giver of Life to the Dead
___ I Will Be What I Will Be	___ Giver of Life to All
___ God the Strong	___ Ruler of the Universe
___ Truth	___ Shepherd of Israel
___ Without End	___ The King of the World
___ Holy One	___ The Place
___ Holiness of Israel	___ *Sh'chinah*
___ King	

Confusing Imagery

For intermediate and advanced contemplation.

Compare many common media images of God, using comics, movie clips, TV shows, paintings, books, etc. What do they have in common? What do they make us think about God? Then study Zeus in Greek mythology. What is similar about Zeus and the common media images? You can have students do a Google image search for "God" and then "Zeus" and compare them.

Then introduce Jewish concepts of God (beyond the anthropomorphic). Include all denominations, and include kabbalistic ideas as well. How are the views different from the common images? Are any of them similar? Add in some of the anthropomorphic texts from the Torah.

Some questions to guide discussion:

- What do these images make you feel?
- Which, if any, can you relate to?
- What are the challenges in depicting God?
- What are the dangers (not physical) in depicting God?
- Are there benefits to using imagery to try to understand God?
- What do you think of when people use the word God? Is there another word for the Divine that you would rather use?
- Why does the Torah use anthropomorphic descriptions of God?

Scaffold: Ask students to consider the last question from many theological standpoints. For example, if the Torah is divine, then why does it use anthropomorphic descriptions of God? If the Torah is written by people, then why are such descriptions used?

God Question Box

For beginner, intermediate, and advanced contemplation.

In advance, write questions about God on index cards, put them in a box, then let students choose a question from the box (either randomly or not) for discussion. You can devote ten minutes per question per class period, or spend an entire period on one question!

Eventually, have students write their own questions and add them to the box for later discussion. This activity teaches that as Jews, we are expected to grapple with difficult issues and ask questions all the time.

Scaffold: Older students can reflect on class discussions in journals or create a God Blog.

Understanding Omniscience

For intermediate and advanced contemplation.

Intermediate: Set up cameras in your classroom (they don't have to be real or working), and announce to students that they will be filmed for the duration of the year. Tell them each film will be reviewed (but never posted anywhere). Do it for at

RESOURCE

For examples of Jewish concepts of God, visit behrmanhouse.com/jec

5

least one day, and then discuss at your next session how it made them feel (some suggested questions are below).

Advanced: Have students set up an experiment: Set up cameras (again, they don't have to be real or working) in a common area of the building that many people use daily. Inform the people walking through the common area that they are being filmed from many angles, and although the film will never be posted anywhere, it will be reviewed and discussed with the class (this information can be conveyed with posted signs). This experiment should last a week or so (or at least two class days). Then they can ask others in the institution some of the following questions, or create their own.

Suggested questions:
- Did your behavior change when you thought you were being watched? If so, why and how? If not, why not?
- In general, how do people's behaviors change when they think they are being watched?
- How did it make you feel to know that everything you did was being filmed and reviewed?
- Was there a time when you stopped thinking about it or didn't care?
- What is challenging about being watched all the time? Why might it be advantageous for us? For society?
- Is it easy or hard to believe that God exists? If God exists and is omniscient, how does that affect one's behavior?

For many students, these kinds of activities and conversations will lead to Jewish lives rich in contemplation and learning.

OTHER BIG IDEAS

Our students of all ages are contemplating serious issues such as, "What's the meaning of life?" "What happens after death?" "Why is there evil in the world?" This is our opportunity to provide a Jewish framework to help them grapple. Whether we are teaching Torah stories, holidays, Jewish history, Jewish values, or practically anything else, we have the perfect opportunity to explore these issues.

Teaching about life-cycle events? This is the time to discuss what Jewish texts and our sages say about love, afterlife, and even the purpose of life. Teaching about Purim and the book of Esther? What a great opportunity to explore the paradox of fate and free will. Studying Rosh Hashanah? Help students debate whether time is truly linear. If it isn't, then what are beginnings? Are there other dimensions? Did God create the concept of time? If so, then what came before time? Even young children think about and can understand some of these ideas. I was eight years old when my father took my brothers and me to see a marathon of *Planet of the Apes* movies (aptly titled, "Go Ape!"). After watching them all (I don't really recommend it), my whole understanding of time was blown out of the water.

How to begin? The key is to find the places in your content that are natural doors to a Big Ideas lesson, discussion, or activity.

Here is a partial list of Big Ideas questions and topics and texts you might use to teach them. This is not, of course, a comprehensive list but a way to help get your mind thinking in this direction. Integrate Big Ideas into your class discussions, questions, game playing, and other activities.

Big Idea	Text, Prayers, Holidays
Meaning of life	Isaiah, Micah, Ecclesiastes, *Pirkei Avot*
Good and evil	All of Genesis, Deuteronomy 30, *Pirkei Avot*
How does God work in this world?	Most of Torah, Jonah, *Pirkei Avot*, Sh'ma, Adon Olam, Pesach/Purim (opposites—revealed and hidden)
What is love?	*V'ahavta l'rei'acha kamocha* (Love your fellow as yourself, Leviticus 19:18), Song of Songs, Ruth, *Pirkei Avot*
Fate or free will?	Esther, *Pirkei Avot*, Yom Kippur, Pesach (Exodus story)
What is reality?	Ecclesiastes, Kabbalah, Shabbat, Shavuot
Is there life after death?	Ecclesiastes, Mishnah, Amidah (traditional version)
What is a soul?	Genesis, Modeh/Modah Ani, Yom Kippur
Is there an objective morality?	*Tanach*, *Pirkei Avot*, Rosh Hashanah, Yom Kippur
What is time?	Ecclesiastes 3, Shabbat, Rosh Chodesh, Rosh Hashanah
What are miracles?	Most of *Tanach*, almost every holiday

• • •

Finding sources and commentaries to show students the breadth of Jewish thought on Big Ideas is important. It grounds them in the ability to form opinions and discuss them confidently. It also helps them realize that Judaism—through our texts, our practices, and our scholars' writings—addresses these issues, and not in a dogmatic or monolithic way.

Some students may need adjustment time to get used to digging deeper. Don't give up! The payoff is worth it.

Ethics ▶6
Pirkei Avot and Beyond

> When I was teaching middle school as a fairly new teacher, my principal came in to evaluate me. Afterward, she said something that I hold dear to this day: "I finally get it. I finally understand why Jewish studies classes are different. You live what you teach. I love math, and I'm passionate about teaching it, but I don't live it. You are living what you are teaching and helping the students live what they learn." She was describing exactly who we Jewish educators are and one of our prime goals. It is different.

Unlike many secular subjects and texts that we might study, everything we teach and learn in the Jewish world is meant to affect us in some way—to change or refine us, and to help us grow. Studying Jewish ethics offers one of the clearest and surest paths. One of the main ways to study Jewish ethics is through *Pirkei Avot* (which translates directly as "Chapters of Our Fathers," but is often translated as "Chapters of Our Sages," "Ethics of Our Fathers "or "Wisdom of Our Sages"). *Pirkei Avot* provides a great resource to help us develop our ethical selves and can lay the foundation for a powerful ethics curriculum.

◆ A Little Educational Philosophy

Judaism has long been considered more than just a religion, and Torah more than just a holy text. Judaism is for many a way of life, a lens through which to view decisions, with the Torah a blueprint for how to examine and understand our very being. In an ancient time of rampant idol worship, child sacrifice, and sketchy morals, Judaism and the Torah provided a strong ethical code and spiritual guidelines. They still do. That's why even today we can connect with the wisdom of our sages.

Even secular educators often want to find a way to teach ethics, convinced, rightly so, of the importance of adding it to their curricula. As Jessica Lahey admits in her essay, "The Benefits of Character Education," "I can't imagine teaching in a school that does not have a hard-core commitment to character education, because I've seen what that education can mean to a child's emotional, moral, and intellectual development. Schools that teach character education report higher academic performance, improved attendance, reduced violence, fewer disciplinary issues, reduction in substance abuse, and less vandalism."[1]

How lucky for us that as Jewish educators we already have the ethical system in place, ready to go. We just need interesting, provocative, and relatable ways to teach it.

⬡ Practical Tools

There are many ways to engage students in ethical studies, discussions, and debates. Here are some ideas for how to begin a dialogue on Jewish ethics and values in general, followed by activity ideas connected to *Pirkei Avot*.

ACTIVITIES TO REINFORCE ETHICS IN GENERAL

Debate an Ethical Issue · *Grades 4 and up*

Have students pair up and research different Jewish opinions using text, commentary, and modern Jewish sources. You might want to assign two pairs to the same issue, one taking the "pro" side and one the "con" side. Each pair should create at least three strong arguments that support their stand. During the debate, give other class members who are watching different roles: jury, timekeeper, witness, etc. Need to save some time? Use *You Be the Judge: A Collection of Ethical Cases and Jewish Answers* by Joel Lurie Grishaver,[2] or *Today's Hot Topics* by Aviva Werner et al.[3] to help.

Values Scavenger Hunt · *Grades 5 and up*

Break students into at least two teams. Ask each team to come up with a list of the seven most important Jewish values (students with strong text backgrounds should provide textual support for their choices). Values might include the importance of family, not gossiping, giving charity, and so on. Teams then swap lists with each other. Each team has a set amount of time to find examples of or create tableaux of these values in action, and take pictures or videos of them. When the teams have collected examples of all the values on their lists, have them share their photos or videos and discuss.

Step Across the Line · *Grades 4 and up*

Gather participants on one side of the room. Using either a physical line or an established imaginary line, have students "step across the line" if they agree completely with (age-appropriate) statements that ask them to take an ethical stand. For example, "Step across the line if you believe that . . . family is important." Start with statements with which everyone can agree, then slowly make them more and more thought provoking. Here are some other statements to use:

- Treating animals cruelly is wrong.
- Human life has value.
- Family is important.
- Children, no matter how old, should always listen to their parents.
- Children, no matter how old, should always do what their parents ask.
- True friendship lasts forever.
- Giving tzedakah shouldn't be optional.
- You should do anything for a friend.
- You should always give money to homeless people who ask.
- You should always give people the benefit of the doubt.
- Gossip can be harmless fun.

After each statement, have any students who stepped over the line go back. This is a silent activity—no discussion or debate just yet.

When they have finished, ask the following questions to lead off a discussion: "Was it frustrating to agree or disagree with an absolute statement?" "Why?" "Were some statements less challenging than others?" Then discuss the actual statements.

An alternative way to play is to make a large outline of a circle instead of a line. Ask people to step into the circle if they agree. Have the circle be small enough that if all the students are in it, it is a little crowded. One of the questions you can ask afterward is, "How did it feel to be out of the circle when almost everyone else was in the circle?" or conversely, "How did it feel to be in the circle when most people were out of the circle?"

CHiP In—The Competing High Priorities Game · *Grades 7 and up*

Life is filled with competing priorities, different values we must think about and assess every time we try to make a moral decision. It's not always obvious which priorities should take precedence as we deal with life's challenges. This Apples-to-Apples-like game asks players to explore the priorities at stake in complicated, real-life situations, and determine which priority should override the others.[4]

Each round, a different player, acting as the judge, reads aloud a card stating a moral dilemma and asks, "What is the highest priority in this situation?" Players must choose from one of their five values chips (out of a possible eighteen values, including Love, Integrity, Power, Education, Family, Health, etc.) and convince the judge that they offer the most compelling reason why their chosen value is the highest priority for that situation. Whoever convinces the judge wins that round and gets the card. Then another person gets to be the judge. This game allows every student to offer an opinion and engage in debate as they explore values clarification. (For more about CHiP In and other card games, see chapter 2.)

What Would You Do Videos · *Grades 3 and up*

Another effective method for provoking discussion is to view videos from the *What Would You Do?* series that ABC News created (available on its website and YouTube). Each video clip features a staged (unbeknownst to the bystanders) scenario that simulates a potentially real situation to see how people nearby would react. The series includes videos that deal with anti-Semitism, racism, and bullying, among other ethical dilemmas. After viewing an age-appropriate clip, have a student lead a discussion about what class members would do, or have students prepare Lens Questions (see chapter 1) for each other. If the students are younger, you can prepare Lens Questions to spur deeper thinking about what they've seen.

ACTIVITIES FOR ANY PIRKEI AVOT CLASS

Artists' Depictions

Have students produce art pieces (either you or they can choose the medium) based on verses from *Pirkei Avot* they have studied. Have them curate their art collection, along with other images and phrases that relate to their verses, to create an art show.

Pirkei Plays

After studying their verses, have students write skits that demonstrate a practical, modern understanding of them. Advanced students can try to construct a whole plot and make a full or one-act play. The plays can either be performed live or filmed and posted on your organization's or school's website.

Poetry Slam

Have students develop poems that help explain or connect emotionally with their verse. They can either perform or illustrate them.

How-to Guide

Students can work in pairs or teams to pick several verses that they feel are most important in our day and age. Have them devise a guide for how to live an ethical life or how to be their best selves featuring the verse, some illustrations, and a description of how the verse applies to them.

Pirkei Avot Games

Create games (see chapter 2) that express the many interpretations and applications of the verses.

Ad Campaigns

After studying several verses, students decide which one is most meaningful to them. They can work in pairs or teams, too. They must campaign for their choice by designing brochures and posters, and making speeches. Afterward, students and teachers can vote.

Pirkei Avot Fair

Hold a Pirkei Avot Fair (see the Proverbs Fair described in chapter 3; use verses from *Pirkei Avot* instead of the book of Proverbs).

We Are Avot

Have learners explore their own ideas regarding what they feel is important and meaningful in life. What wisdom would they like to share? Have students create their own version of *Pirkei Avot*. They can earn extra points for writing their sayings in the style of *Pirkei Avot*.

Try One On

Have students adopt a verse and "live" it for the week. They can keep a journal or blog about their experiences, and should try a new verse each week.

Comic Book Pirkei Avot

Have each student or pair draw a comic to depict a modern-day understanding of their verse. Compile all of their comics into a single book. Make copies for all students to keep and take home.

ACTIVITIES FOR SPECIFIC PIRKEI AVOT VERSES

What Would Aaron Do? · *Pirkei Avot 1:12*

Hillel says: Be of the disciples of Aaron—a lover of peace, a pursuer of peace, one who loves the creatures and draws them close to Torah.

Ask students why Hillel focuses not on Moses, but on his brother Aaron. After exploring what made Aaron special, have students play What Would Aaron Do, described in chapter 2.

Walking in Someone Else's Shoes · *Pirkei Avot 2:5*

Hillel says: Do not separate yourself from the community. Do not believe in yourself until the day you die. Do not judge your fellow until you have stood in his place. Do not say something that is not readily understood in the belief that it will ultimately be understood [or: Do not say something that ought not to be heard even in the strictest confidence, for ultimately it will be heard]. And do not say, "When I free myself of my concerns, I will study," for perhaps you will never free yourself.

Help students see that when we stand in another's place, we learn to empathize rather than judge.

Divide students into teams of two. Give one student a gavel card (use the template at the end of this chapter, for gavel, shoe, and scenario cards) and the other student a shoe card. One team at a time picks a scenario card and reads it aloud. The teammate with the gavel issues a quick judgment of the person in the scenario. The teammate with the shoe card must tell a story about the person in the scenario to explain why we should be more sympathetic. The class then discusses each scenario.

For example, the scenario card says: "You're walking down the street and see a homeless person asking for money."

The student with the gavel might say, "What a lazy slob; he should get a job and stop bothering real people."

The student with the shoes might say, "Maybe that person has just lost his job. It's very hard to find jobs these days. He must be really desperate and lonely. I'm sure it's not easy to ask strangers for money. I don't have much, but I'll try to give him something and at least stop and talk for a minute."

Ask students to contribute any other "shoe" statements. Does the perspective change depending on who wears the shoes (i.e., men, women, or children)?

For each round, have the pair switch shoes and gavel.

The Perfect Friend · *Pirkei Avot 4:18*

Rabbi Shimon ben Elazar says: Do not appease your friend at the height of his anger; do not comfort him while his dead still lies before him; do not ask him about his vow the moment he makes it; and do not endeavor to see him at the time of his degradation.

First have students analyze the verse and try to put it in their own words. How might the verse apply to them? Think of examples. Do they agree or disagree with Rabbi Shimon ben Elazar's ideas?

Working in groups, have students write and perform commercials advertising a product called "The Perfect Friend," based on Rabbi Shimon ben Elazar's saying. They can use their examples to help generate ideas. They could also compare the "perfect" friend with an "imperfect" model. Give them ten to fifteen minutes to work on their commercials. Each group will perform their commercial for the class.

Wise Guy · *Pirkei Avot 5:7*

There are seven things that characterize a fool [uncivilized person], and seven [that characterize] a wise person. A wise person does not speak before one who is greater in wisdom or age, he doesn't interrupt his fellow's words, and he doesn't hasten to answer. [A wise person asks] questions on topic and answers to the point. He responds to first things first and to latter things later. Concerning what he did not hear, he says "I did not hear." He concedes the truth. The opposite [characterizes] the fool.

Ask students to try to read the verses and restate them in more modern terms. They should break them into seven different traits. It might look something like this:

1. The wise person does not speak in the presence of one who is wiser.
2. The wise person does not interrupt when another is speaking.
3. The wise person is not in a hurry to answer.
4. The wise person asks according to the subject and answers according to the Law.

5. The wise person speaks about the first matter first and the last matter last.
6. If there is something the wise person has not heard (and therefore does not know), the wise person says, "I have never heard of it."
7. The wise person acknowledges what is true.

A person who does the opposite of these behaviors is a FOOL!

The students' version or, if you need to save time, the version above can be written on the board or on large sheets of paper posted around the room. Then the game begins.

Divide the group into pairs or small teams. Each team gets eight cards. Seven of those cards have a number on them from 1 to 7, each representing one characteristic of a wise person; the eighth card is labeled "Fool." Read aloud one of the following scenarios and give teams about thirty seconds to decide which of the descriptions of "wise behavior" that scenario describes, or whether it might describe a "fool." When the facilitator calls "cards up," each team holds up its chosen card. Someone can keep score to make it competitive.

The Wise-Guy Game — Scenarios

Scenario 1: George says to his friends, "I think it is important to first decide what we want to do. Then we can decide what time to leave."

Scenario 2: Mrs. Peterson says, "I've never heard of a *pidyon haben* ceremony. But you raise an interesting question, Danielle. I think the rabbi is in her office. Would you mind seeing if she can give you an answer? Then come back and tell us what you found out."

Scenario 3: Dr. Greenberg reaches for the book on his desk that explains different medicines and proper doses. He checks carefully for the correct amount to prescribe for his patient.

Scenario 4: The game show contestant hits the buzzer even before the host finishes speaking and doesn't hear the end of the question.

Scenario 5: The teacher says, "Yes, it's true that we don't know where Moses was buried. We read that in the Torah last week. Why do you think his burial place was kept a secret?"

Scenario 6: Some tourists stop Jack on the street to ask for directions to a new restaurant. Jack doesn't want to seem like he doesn't know his own city very well, so even though he has never heard of this restaurant, he gives them directions.

Scenario 7: At a national science fair, a teacher stands near her student's exhibit, next to the student. When someone asks a question about the display, the teacher says nothing, allowing the student who has done the research to answer.

Scenario 8: Jessica thinks the tour guide might have misquoted something, but she waits patiently until he is done speaking.

Scenario 9: Emily asks, "For *havdalah*, how many candles do we light? I know that for Shabbat, we light two." Rachel answers, "We use just one braided candle for *havdalah*, but it must have at least two wicks."

Scenario 10: Although his older brother, Andrew, is an expert in technology, Josh wants to show that he also knows a lot. So, Josh interrupts his brother, who is explaining to their parents how to fix the computer. Josh tries to finish the explanation himself.

The Wise-Guy Game — Scenario Answer Key

Scenario 1: Trait 5

Scenario 2: Trait 6 (A *pidyon haben* is the "redemption" ceremony that takes place when a firstborn boy is thirty-one days old.)

Scenario 3: Trait 3

Scenario 4: FOOL

Scenario 5: Trait 7

Scenario 6: FOOL

Scenario 7: Trait 1

Scenario 8: Trait 2

Scenario 9: Trait 4

Scenario 10: FOOL

TIP 💡

For advanced students, see if they can do the opposite. Hold up a number and have students come up with a scenario.

• • •

The teachings of *Pirkei Avot* have so much to offer us about the importance of ethical living and using our sages as role models and voices worth contemplating. Luckily for educators, the study of ethics lends itself well to creating engaging games and activities to help students delve into the values and find relevance for their own lives.

Walking in Someone Else's Shoes

Walking in Someone Else's Shoes

SCENARIO CARD

You walk into your classroom in the morning and see a girl crying.

SCENARIO CARD

It's your birthday, but when you come down for breakfast, your mom doesn't wish you a happy birthday.

SCENARIO CARD

You're talking to a group of friends when one of your friends suddenly runs out of the room.

SCENARIO CARD

You tried out for the lead in the school play, but you lost the part to someone else.

SCENARIO CARD

Your teacher seems to be in a bad mood.

SCENARIO CARD

Many of your friends got an invitation to a party in the mail yesterday, but you didn't.

SCENARIO CARD

All of your teachers have scheduled tests or quizzes on the same day.

SCENARIO CARD

You saw a friend of yours, who you know keeps kosher, run into McDonald's.

Maggid ▶ 7
Storytelling for Effective Engagement

I vividly recall the first time I met the wise men of Chelm, my five-year-old self, sitting at our local JCC in rapt attention as I heard the silly way they tried to save the jewels in the snow. From that moment on, I was hooked on Jewish stories.

As an adult, after more than five years of teaching on the West Coast, I began teaching eighth-grade Judaics at a day school in Manhattan. I had developed a strong connection with my California students—deep conversations, spiritual "ah-ha" moments, lots of laughter, and mutual respect. I assumed that I would connect in the same way with my New York students and was stymied when it didn't happen. In fact, they weren't open to anything I had to say or teach. They seemed to dislike me just for being the head of the Judaic Studies Department. How could I fix this? I realized that they didn't know me and didn't trust me. If I were to gain their trust as a Jewish figure, I would have to share my spiritual resume with them—my story of how I came to be who I am and the belief system I carry with me. I would have to become a maggid, a "storyteller." Because my life has been a crazy, funny, and winding journey, I decided I would share my story for five minutes at the start of every class. Of course, I would try to end with some suspense. Slowly, I was able to pull my students in. One day, we didn't have time for the story, and a boy in the class exclaimed, "What? How can you do that to us? This is my soap opera! I have to hear what happens!" Another time, a girl in the class said, "Your life would make a great movie!" Because I told them who I was through a story, they opened up to me and let me into their lives.

Flash forward a few years: I had moved back to the West Coast and was teaching middle-school Jewish history. My students were unruly and had trouble focusing. Once again, I relied on storytelling. At the beginning of each class, I would read from a book about Jews in different historical time periods—the Second Temple, the Middle Ages, the Wild West—and suddenly they calmed down and the Jewish history came alive.

Storytelling can be used to teach lessons in captivating ways, to generate conversations, and to entertain students, but it's also a technique to help students open up to and connect with me. I also use it as an effective classroom management tool (see chapter 14).

Judaism itself begins with a story. Whether Divinely written or inspired, or crafted by humans, the prime tool for teaching about our laws and values and the blueprint for our lives—the Torah—is mostly a grand story filled with imperfect heroes and heroines, various villains, challenging obstacles, important lessons, and lots of drama. What a great way to learn.

◆ A Little Educational Philosophy

Storytelling is one of the most compelling forms of teaching. It opens up listeners' hearts and enables them to think and feel in new ways. In the foreword to the Jewish story collection *Chosen Tales: Stories Told by Jewish Storytellers* (edited by legendary storyteller Peninnah Schram), Rabbi Avi Weiss states, "One can receive a message on an intellectual level, just as one can receive a message on an experiential level. A well-told story is a bridge between the two: it is an attempt to give people a sense of the experience."[1]

A good story hits that sweet spot, as listeners are drawn into hearing lessons even as they are being entertained—*especially* as they are being entertained. This is the secret power of stories. Children are inherently aware of the bridge that stories build between the heart and the mind. That is the beauty of programs like PJ Library, which help young children and their parents connect to Judaism as they connect to each other. But storytelling is no less compelling or important for adults. Rebbe Nachman of Braslov, a Chasidic master of the late eighteenth century, gave over his deepest teachings through storytelling. Today many professional *maggidim* entertain and spark our souls.

Of course, storytelling has a long history in the Jewish tradition. Prolific author and storyteller Dr. Annette Labovitz shares:

RESODURCE

PJ Library is a great resource for children's books on a variety of subjects. Putting together a special reading area in a class with a child-accessible bookshelf and comfy chairs helps facilitate a love and exploration of Jewish stories.

In general, the major goal of storytelling within Jewish tradition is to elevate faith, to inspire people to improve their actions, to teach them "mussar haskel" [ethical understanding]. Stories have been a powerful, motivational, inspirational, educational tool to tell the "happenings" of the Jewish people. Stories have been used to retell our history, to describe our ethics and moral values, to clarify ideas, to help the listener understand specific concepts and ideas, to be an effective instrument to mold and strengthen character, to influence social relationships and draw a portrait of a world to which educators want the learner to relate.[2]

Indeed, every subject in Jewish education can be made more accessible, more powerful, and more inspiring with stories. In fact, you probably noticed that every chapter of this book starts with a story.

⬣ Practical Tools

There are so many ways to use storytelling in the classroom or in informal settings, both reading aloud from written text and telling original stories. Here are some specific ideas to get you started.

Use Stories as Motivation

There are so many inspirational stories in Jewish tradition, and we all have our own personal tales too. For young students, there are a plethora of good, fun stories, usually told in picture-book form, with a message attached. But stories are great for students of all ages, providing jumping-off points for discussions and activities. I've read to fourth graders through adults from *Shlomo's Stories*,[3] the Small Miracles series,[4] and *The Hungry Clothes and Other Jewish Folktales*[5] to inspire and generate good dialogue.

Start Every Class with Storytelling

Students of all ages love to be read to! Spend the first five to ten minutes of every class reading a story as a set induction or introduction to the material you are teaching that day. Read a story at the end of a lesson as a summation of the content students have just learned. Or tell a story that has a connection to the overall theme of the unit or course.

 RESOURCE

Here are some story suggestions for specific topics:

High Holidays: One of my all-time favorite stories, "The Journey of the Lost Princess," from *Chosen Tales* (edited by Peninnah Schram), is a wonderful way to begin a discussion about *t'shuvah* (return, repentance). In it, author Debra Gordon Zaslow blends some traditional elements (Rebbe Nachman of Braslav's story of the

 TIP
Storytelling tips:
- Make eye contact, whether reading a story or telling one. Familiarize yourself with the story, and practice it if necessary, so you are free to connect with the audience.
- Details are important. Create a strong picture for your audience.
- Try out different voices, accents, tones, and vocal variances.
- Consider using a quiet voice occasionally to draw in listeners or create drama. Just make sure that everyone can hear.
- Gauge your speed. If you read or speak too slowly or too quickly, you may lose your audience.
- Use gesture and movement to add to the overall effect.
- Repeat a phrase or movement to anchor a story and keep the listeners' attention.

lost princess) with images from other tales and her own original ideas to create a story that speaks to a huge range of listeners—from kindergarteners through adults. Listeners can tell you about each character—what or whom they represent—as well as discuss the beautiful symbolism.

Non-Biblical Jewish history: This is a subject that really comes alive with stories such as:

- *Hidden: A Child's Story of the Holocaust*, by Loïc Dauvillier, Marc Lizano, and Greg Salsedo (grades 1-5).
- *The Hebrew Kid and the Apache Maiden*, by Robert J. Avrech, about a Jewish family in the American West in the late 1800s (grades 4-8).
- *The Lamp of Darkness*, by Dave Mason with Mike Feuer, an adventure story about a young musician in the Second Temple period (grades 4-adult).
- *The Classic Tales: 4000 Years of Jewish Lore*, by Ellen Frankel, a collection of stories that spans almost all of Jewish history (all ages).

Hebrew: Starting every class reading from a children's picture book is fun way to expose students, even older students, to hearing Hebrew. In addition to wonderful Israeli children's books, you can use Hebrew versions of American classics such as *The Cat in the Hat* and *The Giving Tree*. See what words students know, or if they can figure out the story from the pictures and the way you read it. Are there vocabulary words that repeat? Provide the translation to key words in advance so students can listen for those words, further reinforcing a strong association.

Life-Cycle Events: There are many stories and books on life-cycle events that can lead into meaningful lessons and discussions. For middle school, try *King of the Seventh Grade*, by Barbara Cohen, which deals with both bar mitzvah and conversion (also mild anti-Semitism). I read it to my seventh-grade classes for years. The students were absorbed, they related to the characters, and it always opened up good discussions. Another book of Barbara Cohen's, *Thank You, Jackie Robinson*, deals with dying and death.

Share Personal Stories

TIP
Classroom Management Bonus: Reading to a class or telling a story for the first five to ten minutes helps calm down a rowdy group. Or use stories as a reward: If students focus on the lesson for most of the class, they get a story in the last ten minutes.

Think about the stories of your life—inspirational moments, lessons you learned, amusing anecdotes related to holidays or other Jewish topics. When we share these with our students, we bring them closer to us. We also open the door to hearing their stories. Sharing stories is a great way to develop relationships with our students, as we inspire them and they inspire us.

Hold an informal story slam (such as in podcasts like *The Moth*) where students have to tell a personal story on a topic such as Jewish holidays, tzedakah, encountering God, wrestling with God, *tikun olam*, or Israel, in five minutes or less. The stories can be funny or serious. If you have students who like poetry, this can also be done as a poetry slam.

Encourage Students to Become Storytellers

Students can write (and illustrate) original fiction on any topic you are studying. For example, in my seventh-grade classes, we studied the prophet Elijah as part of a yearlong theme on leadership. I started each class by reading classic Elijah stories. These stories have a certain pattern to them. We discussed how or why Elijah went from the prophet described in the various texts to this mystical folk hero. Then I asked students to write and tell an original Elijah story. The students told beautiful stories and felt that they had contributed in some way to the continuation of this tradition.

Hire a Professional Maggid

There are professional Jewish storytellers—often known as *maggid*-educators—in many cities that add much to any educational program, whether supplementary, day school, youth group, or camp. Giving students a consistent, specific block of time each week to hear a great storyteller, engage in discussion, and even learn how to tell stories can elevate your program and connect students to their Jewish past, present, and future.

Telling Stories in Pairs and Groups

Although traditionally we think of storytelling as one person engaging an audience with a tale, there are also many ways to use storytelling effectively with multiple people. Below are some ideas:

I Say, You Say *(All ages)* After learning any piece of text or Torah, assign each student a different person (or nonhuman or even nonliving item) to embody, and tell the story from different perspectives. Ask students to write a short monologue from that point of view. Have them think about how they felt, what they saw or experienced, and so on. Depending on the age of the learners, you can make the prompts more or less sophisticated. Young students who don't write can just make it up on the spot. Then have everyone perform their monologues, explaining their perspectives.

Example text: When Moses and Aaron go before Pharaoh and announce that swarms of locusts will cover Egypt if the Hebrews are not allowed to leave, Pharaoh's advisors and the people beg him to let the Hebrews go. Pharaoh refuses.

Story Activity: Write the names "Moses," "Aaron," "Pharaoh," "Advisor 1," "Advisor 2," "Egyptian 1," "Egyptian 2," "locust," etc., on pieces of paper. Have students draw a name out of a hat or bowl. Have them take turns sharing

🔍 **RESOURCE**

For a list of professional *maggid*-educators in your area, or to find books for storytelling, such as *Mitzvah Stories: Seeds for Inspiration and Learning* (a collection of stories featuring many great *maggidim*) see reclaimingjudaism.org.

7

❊ CELEBRATING SUCCESS

Jennifer Rudick Zunikoff, a storytelling coach and Jewish educator, taught much of the faculty at the Krieger Schechter Day School in Baltimore how to become storytellers, as well as how to model their new skills for their students. Judaics and secular-studies teachers all learned how to craft stories to reflect and integrate into their curricula. They explored how to inhabit their characters and allow themselves to become vulnerable, which Zunikoff states is the key to a story's success. Lessons became even more engaging, and students were encouraged to follow the model set by their teachers. This was the first success.

The second success was Shuli Raffel's Judaic studies class. She told her sixth graders her personal story of immigrating to Israel from Romania as a very young girl; every listener was transported to Israel back when both Raffel and the country were young. Through their teacher, each student learned of the loneliness and hope that live inside a young refugee trying to belong. The pupils were touched by her vulnerability, as well as the tale itself, and gave her much positive, specific feedback (reflecting the coaching advice on giving affirmations after hearing someone's story).

After Raffel brought her memories to life through storytelling, the students were inspired to research the experiences of their relatives who immigrated to Israel, some in the early 1900s, some after the Holocaust, and some after Israel became a state. Their relatives had immigrated from Yemen, Hungary, Poland, Turkey, and the United States. On Yom Ha'atzma'ut, these students shared their stories with the rest of the middle school. As Raffel recalls, "That day, they became storytellers."

their experiences of what happened. Moses explains his version, Aaron his, the advisors theirs, and so on. Even the locust may have an interesting take on events!

Hebrew Word-at-a-Time Story (*For students with more advanced Hebrew skills*) Use this classic improvisation game to help students use their knowledge of Hebrew words to tell a story. Students sit or stand in a circle. They must tell a cohesive story that is grammatically correct, with each person giving only one Hebrew word at a time. As the story goes around the circle, students have to really listen to each other so that the story makes sense.

Living Museum (*Grades 2 and up*) This storytelling activity brings our past to life and is ideal when you want students to learn about a group of people, such as Jewish sports figures, early Zionist leaders, Prophets, influential Jewish women, modern Jewish heroes, etc.

Students pick a person from a list you've already created. After researching the person—their lives (including their childhoods), their achievements, etc.—students write and deliver monologues, each telling their person's story. Then it's time to create the museum.

Spread everyone throughout a large space, where students can become exhibits about their chosen person. It's fun if they dress like the historic person and use props—either found or created—that their person might have used (such as a small harp for King David or a baseball bat for Sandy Koufax). Students can even create backdrop scenes to put behind their chairs to enhance their exhibits. When visitors (parents, other students, or even community members) stop by, students come to life and tells their first-person stories. When the story is finished, students go back to their original frozen positions until the next visitor arrives.

Story Symphony (*All ages*) Use this improvisation game to review stories from the *Tanach*. Students stand or sit in a circle with the "conductor" (the teacher or group leader) in the middle. The conductor tells the students that they will be reviewing a story that they have learned (e.g., Moses at the burning bush, Joseph interpreting Pharaoh's dreams). The conductor points at a student, who begins the story. Each new person the conductor points to has to continue the story. The conductor should let everyone say a few sentences before picking a new person. If the person was in the middle of a word, the next person must try to pick up where that sentence left off. Students have to really listen to each other and pay attention, because they never know when the conductor will point to them.

● ● ●

Engaging in and teaching students to enter into the deep tradition of Jewish storytelling will add layers of meaning to any Jewish educational experience. Moreover, when we create a Jewish STEM program, consciously adding the elements of spirituality, theology, ethics and *maggid*, we are able to give our students an enjoyable, engaging, thought-provoking, and foundational connection to their own Judaism.

PART THREE

Finding What Works for You: Education Techniques and Approaches

I admit it. I'm the one who jumps on every educational bandwagon. I take the course, read the material, go to the conference, incorporate it in my classroom, and then figure out if it's really all that it's cracked up to be. Usually after trying it, I adjust and alter it to fit my style, my teaching setting, my students, and so on. My main issue with trying to learn most of these techniques is that the examples in the original courses, books, and conferences don't address Judaic subjects or our particular set of challenges. More and more, Jewish educators' conferences and other professional development resources are now focusing on how to bring these techniques into the Jewish education world. But when I first started learning them, I had to figure out for myself how to integrate each approach.

For congregational schools, questions might be: How can I successfully implement a true Project Based Learning unit if my class only meets two and a half hours a week? How can I do Experiential Learning in my classroom since it's not exactly a camp? How can I plan lessons applying Understanding by Design with the limited planning time I have? How can I use Flipped Learning if I'm not supposed to give homework?

For day schools, questions might be: Which methodology is best suited for Judaic studies? How do we transform our existing programs and curricula?

For youth group or camp educators, questions might be: How do classroom-centered methodologies, such as Understanding by Design or Flipped Learning, work in informal educational settings?

Indeed, in the educational world, there are so many methodologies and techniques—some claiming to be the answer to all of our classroom challenges. There are experts and conferences that might introduce us to these new, or not-so-new modalities, but it is still challenging to know which will magically transform, reinvigorate, or refine our programs. This section explores some, but certainly not all, of the most prevalent and successful modalities in education today, each with its champions in both the secular and Jewish education worlds. Thus, it is geared toward both classroom teachers and the educational leaders who support them.

None of the methodologies or approaches here are "either/or"; most of them can be combined in many ways, complementing each other and complementing other techniques not even mentioned here. In fact, every chapter of this book is interconnected—so mix and match! As veteran educators out there know, teaching is all about trial and error, figuring out what works best within our particular set of circumstances.

Use the following list of questions to help choose which method or approach is right for your school, classroom, or program.

- Are there parts of this approach that I can incorporate now?
- Will this approach help serve my greater goals for my class or group?
- Can I adapt it to suit my needs, and how?
- What is the learning curve to successfully using this approach?
- How much training will I or my educators need to feel comfortable and successful?
- What resources are available?
- How accommodating is the space I have?
- Do I have the appropriate technology to make it work? If not, is there a way to adapt it?
- How much time outside of class do I have for planning?
- How can I combine elements of this approach with what I'm currently doing, or with other methods in this book?

Beginning at the End ▶8

Understanding UbD

In the world of secular education, Understanding by Design (UbD) is a commonly used tool for crafting units and lesson plans. Although many universities across the nation teach this methodology for subjects such as math, science, language arts, and social studies, the essence of this approach works well for Jewish education because it emphasizes higher-order thinking and the creation of deeper meanings and connections.

Years ago, when my school sent me to a weeklong UbD conference in Seattle, I experienced a complete paradigm shift. Before then, my lesson plans had consisted of a few scribbled notes describing what I was going to do each class period. I had focused mostly on covering content, and then I would give some sort of assessment—sometimes something creative and sometimes a test. However, at the UbD conference, I realized that I wasn't working to my full potential and figured out how I could fix that. I also learned how to focus and refine all that I was doing right to make it even better. I began putting a lot more effort into all of my lesson plans after that, which helped me become a better educator.

For the next few years, I diligently employed the UbD method in its entirety, staying up late on most evenings to make sure that I got each part perfect. Over the years, though, I have streamlined my process immensely, using the parts of UbD that are most important to me, and I think my students are better for it.

RESOURCE

For a more comprehensive overview and for resources, search "Understanding by Design" at www.ascd.org.

TIP

After using a very thorough, but time-consuming, UbD template for years to craft my curricula, I eventually developed my own modified template, based on the UbD model, other lesson planning templates, and a sense of what works. That template is included in chapter 16.

In Jewish education, when teaching about any text, holiday, ritual, or even historical event, we are always striving to find the deeper idea, lesson, or moral. One of the main goals of UbD is to focus on long-term understanding (knowing it in our "kishkes") over short-term content acquisition. Because we want our students to live their Judaism, not just know about it, UbD's approach is ideal.

So, what is Understanding by Design? It would be impossible in one chapter to encompass the entire UbD method, so let's look at the major components that are most useful for busy educators.

⬢ A Little Educational Philosophy

Educators Grant Wiggins and Jay McTighe developed Understanding by Design, which became nationally recognized in late 1990s. McTighe explains that "effective curriculum development reflects a three-stage design process called 'backward design.' This process helps to avoid the twin problems of 'textbook coverage' and 'activity-oriented' teaching in which no clear priorities and purposes are apparent."[1]

In the sourcebook *The Understanding by Design Guide to Creating High-Quality Units* (ASCD, 2011), the educators assert that "UbD is predicated on the idea that long-term achievement gains are more likely when teachers teach for understanding of transferable concepts and processes while giving learners multiple opportunities to apply their learning in meaningful (i.e., authentic) contexts."

Jewish education is all about wanting our students to "apply their learning in meaningful, authentic contexts." By focusing our lessons on the end goals and understandings first—the ones that might have the most lasting impact—and crafting our sessions around attaining those goals, the experience for our students will be far more effective.

⬢ Practical Tools

UbD curriculum design is composed of three stages:

1. **Desired Results:** Developing the end goals and understandings first.

2. **Evidence:** Using formative and summative assessments (check-ins during and at the end of the learning).

3. **Learning Plan:** Creating the actual lesson plans.

This chapter focuses largely on the first and second stages. See chapter 16 to learn about creating lesson plans using an adapted model of UbD.

DESIRED RESULTS

Whether planning for the whole year, a unit, or a lesson within a unit, understanding is the goal. Focus on helping students apply what they have learned to various circumstances, showing that the knowledge is real and lasting. This is accomplished through what's referred to as Enduring Understandings and Essential Questions.

Enduring Understandings (EUs) are not facts—that will come later—but rather the accumulated wisdom that comes from examining, experiencing, and recognizing some important new, relevant idea. For each unit of study, three to five EUs are plenty. Each lesson within the unit also has its Enduring Understandings. A lesson may take more than one class period, but it is focused on a more specific idea, piece of text, ritual, or concept within the larger unit. Because it is more focused, one or two EUs are all that are needed for the lesson.

Essential Questions (EQs) are open-ended inquiries that lead students to engage actively in a topic or EU. There are usually one or two corresponding EQs for every EU.

Examples of Enduring Understandings and Essential Questions

Example 1: Introduction to Tanach · *Grades 3 and up*

Enduring Understandings:

1. *Tanach* is a tool we can use to learn about life and how to live it.

2. In studying Jewish texts, asking questions is an essential part of the learning process.

3. Seeing more than one side to any part of the *Tanach* allows more depth of knowledge.

4. The *Tanach* connects us with our past, but it isn't meant to be a history book.

5. Torah can point the way to how we can come closer to the Divine ideal.

Essential Questions:

1. How is learning Torah like learning math, science, history, etc.? Why might it be different? Why might it be similar?

2. What are the most efficient ways to learn? Why is asking questions so important for learning anything? What kinds of questions will help most in learning *Tanach*?

3. What does the saying "There are two sides to every story" mean? Can there be more than two sides? Can there be only one side? How? Why is it important to examine many angles?

4. How might it be dangerous or helpful to study *Tanach* as a history book? Would we be the "Jewish people" without the Torah? Why or why not?

5. What would God's ideal world be like? Is it the same as our real world?

NOTE

There are not always universally accepted understandings of Jewish concepts and texts. You may or may not agree with the EUs or EQs used in the examples. The goal is simply to show how they work.

8

NOTE

Notice how each EU has a corresponding set of EQs that relate to it.

Example 2: God and Rosh Hashanah · *Grades 7 and up*

Enduring Understandings:

1. Judaism encourages us to struggle, if necessary, to try to understand the unknowable.

2. Anthropomorphic descriptions of God are not meant to be literal but only to explain God in terms we can understand.

3. The Torah is not a history book but a blueprint for how to live our lives.

4. Our finite minds cannot understand all the doings of the infinite.

5. The concept of time is an amazing gift.

Essential Questions:

1. How can we try to understand the unknowable?

2. What does God look like?

3. What is the point of having the Torah? How does it connect us with God?

4. How can we imagine something we've never seen or experienced? Is it possible?

5. What would a world be like without the concept of time?

Example 3: The Spies Bring Back a Bad Report · *Grades 5 and up*

Enduring Understanding:
The way others treat us is often a reflection of how we feel about ourselves.

Essential Question:
How do we affect the way others treat us?

Example 4: Shabbat Rituals · *Grades K-4*

Enduring Understandings:

1. Rituals are the things we do to connect us to our past, to the Jewish people, to our families, and to God.

2. In Judaism, lighting candles is a way to separate different times in a special way.

Essential Questions:

1. How do rituals help us on Shabbat? In what way do rituals make us feel close to our families? To the Jewish people? To God? (Note that we don't ask, "What are the rituals we do on Shabbat?" because that is a closed-ended question. The answers certainly have their place in the teaching of this lesson, but not as EQs.)

2. What does light represent? (For really young students: What happens when we light candles? How does it make you feel?)

Example 5: Introduction to Prayer · *Grades 3 and up*

Enduring Understandings:

1. There are many kinds of prayers.

2. Prayer can affect us in positive ways.

3. The Sh'ma is the defining Jewish prayer.

4. Prayer is a way that Jewish people have used to connect with God throughout history.

Essential Questions:

1. What is prayer? Why do people pray? When do people pray?

2. Can prayer effect change? If so, how?

3. What prayer says "This is Judaism" to you? What does the "Oneness" of God really mean? (It is more than possible that students will have other interesting answers to the question, "What prayer says 'This is Judaism' to you?" That is great, too! It can start a wonderful conversation. An Essential Question should be open-ended and not a leading question for the one answer you want. If this is a younger class, the third question might not apply at all, since they won't yet have knowledge of many prayers.)

4. How have the Jewish people connected to God throughout history?

Other ways to use EUs and EQs

Asking EQs is a great way to begin a lesson (see the set inductions section of chapter 16), or you can post them around the room for reflection, and ask them at different points.

EUs can also be posted around the room or handed out at the beginning of a unit. They can also be used as a source of reflection or not explicitly shared at all.

The key to writing strong EUs and EQs, in addition to practice, is to make sure that they don't reflect knowledge or facts, and that questions are open-ended so you can facilitate discussion. However, this doesn't mean that knowledge, facts, and skills aren't important; just focus on them after you have figured out your EUs .

Knowledge, Skills, and Goals

Developing the EUs and EQs for a particular topic sets us up to consider what knowledge, skills, and goals are required for students to reach those desired results.

There is so much we want our students to know about Judaism. What **knowledge**—facts and basic concepts—do we want our students to comprehend and recall?

We also want to empower them with many **skills** (which they will master over time), including reading Hebrew, saying prayers, and participating in rituals. But skills can also refer to 21st century classroom skills—collaboration, creativity, critical thinking, etc. So even if a lesson doesn't have a particular emphasis on tangible skills like reciting a blessing or decoding Hebrew, it may address other important areas, such creative problem solving or asking analytical questions.

Goals are the big-picture objectives that prompt inquiry, thought, and exploration of a topic. They are phrased with active verbs, expressing what we want our students to accomplish, and are usually related to our EUs and EQs.

Let's look at how we can extend those EU/EQ examples to add in the knowledge, skills, and goals we want as our student focus.

Example 1: Introduction to Tanach

Students will know:

- The sections of the *Tanach*—Torah, Prophets, and Writings—and which books are in each.
- Who the different commentators are (older grades).
- The basic layout of a page of *Tanach* (which is the main text, which are the comments).
- Basic biblical Hebrew grammar (day-school students).

Students will be skilled at:

- Finding chapters and verses.
- Decoding Hebrew and translating a few key words.
- Translating verses from Hebrew (day-school students).

Goals—Students will:

- Examine and debate the structure of the *Tanach*.
- Compare the structure of *Tanach* to history books and discuss the differences.
- Explore the various ways we can use the *Tanach* as a guide for our lives.

Example 2: God and Rosh Hashanah

Students will know:

- Rules for engaging in respectful dialogue.
- The different names for God and when they are used.
- Rosh Hashanah customs and traditions.
- The translation of the prayer Avinu Malkeinu.
- The translation of the prayer Al Cheit.
- The meaning of *t'shuvah* (returning to one's better self).

Students will be skilled at:

- Respectful dialogue.
- Supporting their opinions.
- Decoding Hebrew and translating key words in Avinu Malkeinu and Al Cheit.
- Analyzing text from the Torah.

Goals—Students will:

- Grapple with the paradox of trying to know the unknowable.

- Debate the purpose of Torah and how it might/might not connect us with God.
- Explore Rosh Hashanah prayers and find personal meaning.
- Connect to the opportunities inherent in starting over on Rosh Hashanah.
- Consider the challenges of starting over on Rosh Hashanah.

Example 3: The Spies Bring Back a Bad Report

Students will know:
- Basic story of the text, Numbers 13.
- Some of the commentators' ideas on the text.

Students will be skilled at:
- Decoding the text and translating a few key words.

Goals—Students will:
- Feel empowered by understanding the relationship between these verses and self-esteem.
- Find correlations between the Torah and their own lives.

Example 4: Shabbat Rituals

Students will know:
- The Shabbat rituals involving the candles, wine, and challah.
- A variety of rituals, including washing hands before blessing the challah and various Shabbat songs.
- That *havdalah* means "separation" and that the Havdalah ceremony separates Shabbat from the rest of the week.

Students will be skilled at:
- Reciting the blessings over the candles, wine, washing of hands, and challah.
- Singing L'cha Dodi to different tunes.

Goals—Students will:
- Explore and experience different Shabbat rituals and their meanings.
- Examine the use of light and candles in Jewish practice and connect it to the idea of time.
- Sing various Shabbat songs that they can share with their families.

Example 5: Introduction to Prayer

Students will know:
- The basic structure of the prayer service.
- The construct of blessings (*Baruch Atah*, etc.).
- The basic history of the Amidah.
- The translation of the Sh'ma and V'ahavta.

Students will be skilled at:
- Saying basic prayers, including parts of the Amidah.
- Reciting the Sh'ma and V'ahavta.

Goals—Students will:
- Debate the importance of having a set order to prayer.
- Discuss what the "Oneness" of God might mean and come up with a personal connection to the concept.
- Find their own personal way to connect with prayer.

EVIDENCE

The second stage of designing UbD curriculum is Evidence. How will we know whether students have truly internalized the EUs and acquired the necessary knowledge and skills that we laid out in stage 1, Desired Results? Relying on a combination of formative and summative assessments will let us know both where the students are in their comprehension of material and, more importantly, whether they can analyze, apply, and integrate it. Although there are many types of assessments that help check for understanding as well as acquisition of knowledge and skills, here we will focus only on GRASPS, a mainstay of UbD assessments. (For a more in-depth look at assessments, please see chapter 15.)

GRASPS

GRASPS is a method for planning and crafting summative assessments that fully engage students in the application of EUs. It also includes a demonstration of knowledge and skills. Because the assessment is goal oriented, students have a reason to integrate all that they have learned to solve the problem, task, or challenge. GRASPS also helps students develop critical-thinking skills as they apply what they have learned. Here is the explanation of the acronym and two examples for using this tool.

Goal: Provide a statement of the task. Establish the goal, problem, challenge, or obstacle in the task.

Role: Define the role of the students in the task. State the job of the students to meet the task.

Audience: Identify the target audience within the context of the scenario. Example audiences might include a client or committee.

Situation: Set the scene. Explain the situation.

Products or Performances: Clarify what the students will create and why they will create it.

Standards and Criteria: Provide students with a clear picture of success. Identify specific standards for success. Issue rubrics to the students or develop them with the students.[2]

When planning a GRASPS assessment, the order of the elements is not important. I try to write my GRASPS assessments as narratives because that is my style, but they can be written in list form or in any other way that suits you. In the examples below, I start with the Role, followed by the Situation. Each section is labeled to indicate which part of GRASPS is being used.

Example 3: The Spies Bring Back a Bad Report

You are an out-of-work writer. *(Role)*

You have been looking on Craigslist (or a local paper) for a job and think you might have found the perfect one. Here is what the ad says:

> *The popular Jewish advice columnist for the Torah Times, Dear Sage, is retiring. Our paper is looking for a compassionate, humorous new columnist, who can help readers with their problems by incorporating lessons from the Torah. Potential candidates should e-mail us an answer to one of the reader's questions below. (Situation)*

E-mail 1:

> *Dear Sage,*
>
> *I am a fourteen-year-old girl who doesn't feel very good about herself. I don't think I'm ugly, but when I went to the dance the other night with my friend, all the boys asked her to dance and not me. Even though she isn't really prettier or nicer than me, she danced all night with a smile on her face, while I sat in the corner moping. I don't know why nobody asked me to dance. What should I do?*
>
> *—Ms. Wallflower*

E-mail 2:

> *Dear Sage,*
>
> *I am a thirteen-year-old boy, and I want to be taller. My parents keep telling me to be patient because I'll grow soon. But I'm tired of all the jokes. I'm afraid that the girls will only like the tall guys, even though my best friend is shorter than me, and girls always like him and laugh at his jokes. It doesn't seem fair that other guys are so much taller. I feel like a total loser. What should I do?*
>
> *—The Kosher Shrimp*

After choosing which e-mail to answer, you are very excited about using your knowledge of the spies to provide good advice and get this great, high-paying job! *(Goal)*

You type your answer *(Product)* for the publisher *(Audience)*, making sure to incorporate a verse from the text since the *Torah Times* needs to see how you use the Torah to give advice. Don't forget to use proper spelling, grammar, and punctuation or you won't get hired. *(Standards)*

Example 4: Shabbat Rituals

You are travelers from a far-off planet called Tabash, sent to find out about life on Earth. *(Role)* Many of the fellow beings on your planet are really mean, and you are looking for a better way of life for you and your friends and family. You think studying the way of life on Earth might persuade mean Tabashians to change. You've heard good things about Shabbat and Judaism, and have come to check them out. You love the idea of a day of rest and have discovered many Shabbat rituals that you think seem quite meaningful. *(Situation)*

You must prepare a booklet *(Product)* to explain all of the rituals so that the Tabashians *(Audience)* will want to begin celebrating Shabbat, perform the rituals, and, hopefully, feel less stressed out and become kinder to each other. *(Goal)*

For each ritual, make sure to explain what it is, how to do it, and how it is connected to Shabbat. If you've tried any of the rituals, explain how it felt to do them. And don't forget to illustrate your booklet. *(Standards)*

● ● ●

Using and mastering these essential elements of UbD will help create a more in-depth and meaningful learning experience for your students. The EUs and EQs drive the lesson's activities, which in turn guide your students to integrate what they've learned and show successful evidence of such learning in creative ways. Your students will reap many benefits as you become more adept at crafting EUs, EQs, and GRASPSs, while incorporating other techniques, methodologies, and practices.

NOTE

For younger students who don't write yet, ask them to demonstrate the rituals for the Tabashians back on their planet and explain them. The Tabashians can be other adults, including the rabbi and cantor, and /or their classmates. As each group performs their demonstration, it will also reinforce the concepts.

More than Just Projects ▶**9**
Project Based Learning

When I first heard the term "Project Based Learning," I thought it would be right up my alley! After all, like many educators out there, I love to use projects in my classes. With all the cool projects my classes have done over the years, I was shocked to learn that I was not actually doing Project Based Learning (PBL) at all—it was just using projects to learn. Sometimes, we would make a project as the "fun part" of a unit. More often, however, I would use the project as a creative assessment (more on this in chapter 15)—a way of checking for deeper understanding. These are both legitimate and often very successful uses of projects, but neither is actually PBL. In fact, only once did I actually do a PBL-type unit (unbeknownst to me at the time). So now that we know what it isn't, let's look at what it is, and what it can do for you and your students.

Here is how the Buck Institute for Education (one of the leading voices in the PBL movement) describes it: "Project Based Learning is a systematic teaching method that engages students in learning important knowledge and developing 21st century competencies through an extended, student-influenced inquiry process structured around complex, authentic questions and carefully designed products and learning tasks."[1]

What does this mean in a Jewish educational context? We want students to explore meaningful, relevant questions that arouse curiosity. The flow of questions and answers will lead to students creating personal Jewish connections while they engage in important core life skills, such as collaboration, analytical inquiry, and using technology. The product or project is not the end of the learning—it is the reason for engaging in the learning. The product is an authentic representation of students' grappling with the questions and the answers they have invested with their time.

⬢ A Little Educational Philosophy

Teachers and administrators in the secular education world are increasingly using PBL as they discover its power to make school more engaging for students. "In PBL, students are active, not passive; a project engages their hearts and minds, and provides real-world relevance for learning."[2] Additionally, with PBL, teachers are better able to scaffold learning, incorporate technology and creativity, and "work more closely with active, engaged students doing high-quality, meaningful work, and in many cases rediscover the joy of learning alongside their students."[3] Which all sounds wonderful. But it does take a great deal of strong professional development, and a serious commitment, to implement successfully.

For many reasons—including lack of time for training and implementation, and budget constraints that preclude serious professional development in PBL—it hasn't caught on as quickly in the Jewish educational world. But there's real value in trying PBL in Jewish educational programs because, "the methodology moves students from the traditional Hebrew school setting of listening about Judaism to 'really engaging in Judaism and taking ownership of it,'" according to Anna Marx, project director for Shinui: The Network for Innovation in Part-Time Jewish Education.[4] Some Jewish programs that have experimented with this approach have either completely moved to a PBL model or have incorporated many PBL elements, which is sometimes goal enough.

This engaging methodology offers another way to help our students connect and immerse themselves in their Jewish educations.

⬢ Practical Tools

Before we examine a more detailed, step-by-step understanding of PBL, with concrete examples, let's note two issues.

First, it is not possible in the breadth of one chapter to convey an in-depth exploration of Project Based Learning. For more detailed information, see BIE.org (Buck Institute for Education's website for great resources, tutorials and more) and Edutopia.org (more excellent resources and tutorials). If you are able to get to a PBL conference, all the better.

Second, because of various challenges in the many Jewish educational settings in which we operate, we often are not able to implement full, Gold Standard PBL (more on this later). That's okay! Even if you are able to incorporate some of the elements, you will still see positive results, such as an increase in critical-thinking skills and higher student engagement.

If you are a veteran of PBL or have already begun to incorporate elements of it into your curriculum, skim this chapter for future lesson ideas, new inspiration, and as a refresher of all the elements.

ELEMENTS OF PROJECT BASED LEARNING

Project Based Learning uses focused inquiry to help students uncover the content, knowledge, skills, and understandings that you want them to gain. In Gold Standard PBL (meaning the most complete and best version), the following eight elements are present:

1. Key Knowledge, Understanding, and Success Skills
2. Challenging Problem or Driving Question
3. Sustained Inquiry
4. Authenticity
5. Student Voice and Choice
6. Reflection
7. Critique and Revision
8. Public Product

When you're just beginning to create a PBL environment, however, trying to make sure you hit every element perfectly is daunting and likely unrealistic. Experimenting with PBL is a worthy and accessible goal in and of itself, so add and combine the different elements as you can. Incorporate them slowly into your lessons, and eventually you and your class will be ready for a full PBL unit.

Let's look at each element and examples of it in action.

Key Knowledge, Understanding, and Success Skills

What knowledge do we want students to acquire?

What are the key understandings we want them to get from a particular unit of study? In well-constructed project ideas, students will be able to apply these concepts and understandings to real-world or authentic problems or questions.

What success skills will they need? Think about including critical thinking and other twenty-first-century skills.

Here is an example of how we might express this PBL element in a unit on *t'filah* for fifth or sixth grade:

Knowledge to acquire:
- Common vocabulary.
- Various tunes.
- Where different prayers come from, who wrote them, and when.
- Different traditions (from various Jewish denominations and from diverse cultures).

Key concepts and understandings:
- *T'filah* is a way to connect and engage in a relationship with God.
- *T'filah* has changed over time.
- *T'filah* can transform us.
- The prayer service has a purposeful and intentional order.

NOTE

Aren't these terms also found in Understanding by Design? Yes! Here's the translation:

PBL: Key concepts and understanding
UbD: Enduring Understandings

PBL: Success skills
UbD: Skills

PBL: Knowledge
UbD: Knowledge

9

Success Skills:
- Ability to think critically about the prayers we say.
- Ability to analyze the prayers.
- Mastery of the words of key prayers.

Challenging Problem or Driving Question

The **Driving Question** propels the entire PBL unit. This is the heart of a project—the problem to investigate or the question to answer. The Driving Question should provoke more questions and create a desire in students to investigate further. It can be a concrete, task-oriented question or a more abstract, debatable question.

Concrete, task-oriented questions usually incorporate the Product. For example, "How can we create a more personal siddur to help us and others connect to God?" The product is the siddur, and the question prompts the reflection, discussion, inquiry, and discovery necessary to create the product.

On the other hand, abstract questions leave more room for Student Voice and Choice, another important PBL element that allows more student ownership and connectivity. For example, "Why do Jews pray?" is an abstract question. Note that there is no specific task mentioned. Students might then decide (Voice and Choice) what the task and product will be that will help them answer this question.

A good Driving Question is:
- relatable
- engaging
- authentic (meaning real-world or relevant)
- one that leads to further sustained inquiry
- challenging but not intimidating for students

Each PBL unit will have *only one* Driving Question. However, each of the following examples shows at least one concrete and one abstract question per topic to demonstrate how any unit can be scaffolded to fit your needs. As you decide what kind of question—concrete or abstract—is best for your class, consider factors such as the age of your students, class time available, students' personal desire, and overall goals of the lesson.

Example 1: Tzedakah

Concrete Driving Question: How can we make the biggest impact with $1000?
Abstract Driving Question: What is the most meaningful way of fulfilling the mitzvah of tzedakah?

Example 2: T'filah

Concrete: How can we create a more personal siddur to help us and others connect to God? Or: What would be the ideal prayer space?
Abstract: Why do Jews pray? Or: Does prayer work?

Example 3: Jewish History

Concrete: How can we create an interactive Jewish history timeline that will help non-Jews understand the relationship between Jewish history and world history?

Abstract: What is the most pivotal point in modern/ancient Jewish history?

Example 4: Tanach

Concrete: How can we create a guide to marriage based on the successful and not-so-successful models from *Tanach*?

Abstract: Who is the greatest Jewish leader in *Tanach*?

Example 5: Israel

Concrete: How can we produce a podcast about life in Israel to share a side that many in the non-Jewish community don't get to see?

Abstract: What is the most influential city in Israel?

Example 6: Holidays

Concrete: How can we create a haggadah for young children to help them better understand and participate in the seder (grade 5 and up)? Or: How can we create a comic book about the story and customs of Chanukah (any grade)?

Abstract: Which Jewish holiday is most important? Or: How can celebrating Rosh Hashanah improve our year?

Example 7: Shabbat

Concrete: How can we make a meaningful Shabbat dinner experience for our parents?

Abstract: What can we gain from celebrating Shabbat?

After developing the Driving Question, you can design your unit (use the template at the end of this chapter for guidance), incorporating the rest of the PBL elements.

As we explore the rest of the elements, we will revisit these driving questions to expand on the examples.

Entry Event

Although this is not one of the eight elements of Gold Standard PBL, it is a crucial part of the planning process. The entry event is the important kickoff to your unit that should grab students' attention and get their questions and imaginations percolating. Videos, films, experts in the field, activities, and field trips are all great entry events because they provoke inquiry. Often students' questions and discussions on an entry event can lead to finessing the Driving Question or help steer the next steps of the process. After the entry event, students can work in pairs or groups for the rest of the unit.

TIP

If you ever get stumped trying to come up with a Driving Question, here is a simple formula: *How can we as __A__ create a __B__ to help __C__ address/do/change __D__?* Remember, the more real-world or relevant the Driving Question is for students, the more they will enthusiastically explore.

Example 1: How can we as fifth-grade students create a way to explain the seder for young children so they can get the most out of their home seders?

Note: This is similar to "How can we create a haggadah for young children to help them better understand and participate in the seder?" However, the former question leaves more choice for what the actual product will be. The latter has more specific goals, but both address a real-world problem that older students can relate to—engaging children, including themselves, in seders.

Example 2: How can we, as tour guides, plan a tour of our synagogue to show visitors what we value?

Not every question has to follow the formula exactly, and often students can help create the final driving question.

9

Sustained Inquiry

After the Entry Event, students begin asking questions and investigating—a process that takes time, more than a few days or classes. Begin by having students generate questions based on the Driving Question. Each of those questions might lead to more questions. You can have students keep track of their questions in a journal or online, using mind-mapping software like Inspiration, which provides graphic tools. Here's an example below.

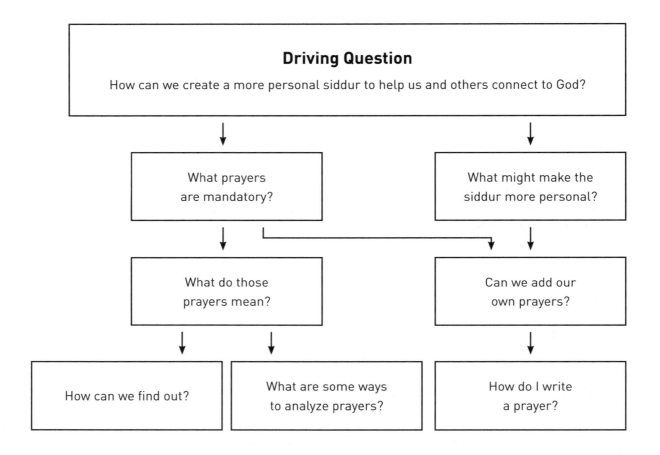

Driving Question

How can we create a more personal siddur to help us and others connect to God?

What prayers are mandatory?

What might make the siddur more personal?

What do those prayers mean?

Can we add our own prayers?

How can we find out?

What are some ways to analyze prayers?

How do I write a prayer?

Although these are simply examples of questions students may or may not imagine on their own, even if you provide these early questions, each one can potentially lead to many more questions. After an initial question brainstorming session, students can and should be encouraged to continue to add questions throughout the project.

As students begin to ask questions, they will also investigate answers. You will probably have to help them find resources, especially younger students. Sometimes, you might want to have a lesson that relates to their questions or set up learning opportunities for them. Flexibility on the teacher's part to follow students' leads helps create a sense of ownership for the students.

Authenticity

In PBL lingo, "authentic" doesn't mean real or genuine, but instead refers to real-world applicability. There are several ways for a project to be authentic; you can choose just one or combine them.

Authentic Context: Students answer problems beyond the classroom.
Examples:
- Developing a business plan for a new Jewish-themed product.
- Designing a public prayer space.
- Recommending policy to combat anti-Semitism to the local government.

Real-World Tools, Task, or Process: Students use real technology, whether digital or workshop-type tools, to create their project. The process itself is a real-life process. They may have to learn new skills to complete the project.
Examples:
- Creating and filming a newscast on current events that affect the Jewish world (or local Jewish community).
- Designing a digital game or app that incorporates Jewish ideas or themes.
- Building a fantasy sukkah for the congregation.

Impact on Others: Students address a need for their school, community, or elsewhere. The project is something that will be used or experienced by others.
Examples:
- Creating a new prayer book for the congregation to use at special family Shabbat services.
- Creating a haggadah for young children.
- Making a meaningful Shabbat experience for parents.
- Putting together kits to use when visiting the sick (*bikur cholim*)

Personal Authenticity: The project relates to students' interests, identities, or concerns. Jessica Lahey, in a *New York Times* article, affirms,

> *Great teachers understand that the best, most durable learning happens when content sparks interest, when it is relevant to a child's life, and when the students form an emotional bond with either the subject at hand or the teacher in front of them. Meaningful learning happens when teachers are able to create an emotional connection to what might otherwise remain abstract concepts, ideas or skills.*[5]

Examples:
- Creating a personal siddur.
- Cooking a food particular to a student's heritage/culture as part of a larger meal.
- Making a Public Service Announcement for a Jewish organization or cause that has meaning for a student.

9

Student Voice and Choice

Giving students some say in a project gives them a sense of ownership. As a result, they will give more of themselves. Focus, enthusiasm, and effort will come more naturally and easily. Students need to be able to use their judgment, ask questions, and perhaps have some input on the project concept itself. Consider the age of the students and their familiarity with PBL culture and/or independent learning when determining how much of the project you will have to map out and how much voice and choice you can give.

If you have second graders, you will have to come up with the Driving Question, the resources for gathering the information, the format of the learning, the schedule, and possibly the final project. The students can help you develop the schedule, ask questions, and perhaps give ideas for the project (especially if they've done a PBL unit before).

An eighth-grade class can probably help you come up with the schedule, make suggestions for resources, and choose the project.

Wherever possible within the other PBL elements mentioned here, try to find places that can offer students a voice and choice to help them take ownership of their projects. With proper reflection and critique, you can help students stay on track if their choices lead them astray.

Reflection

This is critical to the PBL process. As the great education philosopher John Dewey famously stated, "We do not learn from experience. We learn from reflecting on experience." Both you and your students should continually reflect on what is being learned, how it is being learned, and why it is being learned. These reflections should happen in both formal and informal ways throughout the whole process. Reflections are part of the classroom culture through dialogues and discussions at various checkpoints, and they help in the final assessment of the project. Remember that obstacles and failures are valuable learning tools if we can reflect on and grow from them.

Examples:
- Student journals, logs, or blogs
- Student interviews with each other
- Group reflection or intergroup feedback (groups reflecting on other groups) using either of the following:
    1. This great rule: "Be kind. Be specific. Be helpful."[6]
    2. The "I like _____. I wonder _____" model (e.g., "I like the way you created the illustrations for your haggadah. I wonder if the explanations might confuse a younger child.")
- Invite experts to visit and provide feedback
- Older students helping younger students
- Questions focused on specific aspects of the process
- For younger students: Charts with stickers describing how they feel

Critique and Revision

For students to feel accomplished, their PBL unit should be of the highest quality. Providing constructive feedback from peers, from you, and possibly even outside experts helps students improve and learn how to revise their work. If necessary, students can be taught how to give and receive constructive peer feedback. This is the perfect opportunity to teach and reflect on *mitzvot* and Jewish values that can inform this instruction: not embarrassing someone in public, offering rebuke from the heart, humility, not putting a stumbling block before the blind, and so on.

Public Product

The product itself can be whatever your students create, whether it exists in physical space, virtual space, or a performance. Here are some ideas.

Physical
- Brochure/ pamphlet
- Game
- Exhibit
- Artwork
- Siddur
- Haggadah
- Food
- Book
- Magazine
- Blueprint
- Model
- Artifacts
- Curated space

Virtual/Intangible
- Website
- Blog
- Vlog
- Event

Performance
- Song
- Concert
- Poetry
- Poetry slam
- Podcast
- Play
- Public Service Announcement video
- Webisode
- Web series
- Newscast
- Storytelling
- Presentation
- Debate

Here is the really important part: the "public" of Public Product. Whatever the product, it must be presented in some way to a forum or audience outside of the class and teacher. When the stakes are much higher, the work will be stronger. As much as possible, the "audience" should somehow be connected to the project and product. Below are some ideas for public audiences using some of our previous examples:

Driving Question	Public Product and Audience
How can we make the biggest impact with $1000?	Create a business proposal; present the findings and goals to a panel of experts/parents/Federation members.
How can we create a more personal siddur to help us and others connect to God?	Develop a siddur that uses photos and artwork. Each student or group has his or her own. Use them in services with family and friends. Perhaps sell some online to raise money.
What would be the ideal prayer space?	Depict it in a model, blueprint, or brochure presented to synagogue board members or a group of architects.

Driving Question	Public Product and Audience
How can we create an interactive Jewish history timeline that will help non-Jews understand the relationship between Jewish history and world history?	Create an interactive Jewish history timeline as a website or app that is available to the public. Or have students perform, creating scenes from Jewish history on a "live timeline" with which people can interact. Create tableaux; invite an interfaith group.
What is the most pivotal point in modern/ancient Jewish history?	Debate before a panel of Jewish history experts or other judges.
How can we create a guide to marriage based on the successful and not-so-successful models from *Tanach*?	Create *The Tanach's Guide to Marriage*, a pamphlet, booklet, or magazine distributed to the public. Or present to rabbinical leaders or marriage counselors.
How can we produce a podcast about life in Israel?	A podcast for the non-Jewish community about life in Israel, giving them a perspective on Israel that they don't hear about in the news.
What is the most influential city in Israel?	Brochures or a presentation to prospective tourists (students or adults) to Israel. Or a debate for a panel of tour guides and travel agents.
How can we create a haggadah for young children to help them better understand and participate in the seder?	A haggadah that can be used in a model seder for younger students and then taken home for use at their family Passover celebration.
How can we make a meaningful Shabbat dinner experience for our parents?	Students help prepare Shabbat foods, set the table, or make a blessings/song booklet for a special communal family Shabbat meal. Parents can take home the booklets for future use.
What can we gain from celebrating Shabbat?	Students keep a blog or vlog and try out different ways to celebrate Shabbat or Shabbat mitzvot. They record the vlog or make blog entries after Shabbat that relate their experiences and post them on the school or synagogue website.
What would be the perfect Jewish community?	Students create a large model, brochures, or travel posters of their ideal Jewish community and exhibit it/ them at their local JCC, Federation, or other community organization.

BEFORE GETTING STARTED

Keep in mind that implementing a full PBL unit successfully takes time and practice. Most of us have time challenges, whether we're at a congregational program or a day school, so approach PBL by gradually adding elements of it to your curriculum— perhaps modifying a single unit. Remember that a well-constructed PBL unit can cover many curricular objectives at once. For example, the sample unit outlined below can be scaffolded to include Hebrew decoding and translation practice, learning *t'filah* (both the actual prayers and the deeper personal connections we can make with them) and history, as well as twenty-first-century technology skills.

NOTE

What is the teacher's role in a PBL unit? After designing the PBL unit, you are a "facilitator of knowledge" rather than the traditional "giver of knowledge." Teachers are like coaches and mentors, curating activities, learning experiences, and opportunities that will help students in their inquiries and with their products. Depending on the age and experience of the students, you can adjust your levels of interaction and content delivery. Encourage questions, and try to guide students to find the answers. Offer feedback every step of the way.

TIP

Whether you're a beginner or an expert, self-reflection is crucial after trying any PBL unit, modified or not. What worked? Why did it work? Can it be duplicated in future attempts? What didn't work as well? Why didn't it work? How can these pitfalls be avoided in the future? What needs to be tweaked or refined? As we might remind our students, failing is a powerful tool that can lead us to success. So it goes for us, as well!

A Sample PBL Unit

Below is a completed outline of a PBL unit, "Personal Picture Siddur," followed by a blank template form you can use to create your own PBL units. (Blank forms can be downloaded at www.behrmanhouse.com/jec.) Use this lesson as is or modify it for your needs. Perhaps modeling how to use the template will spark a different idea.

This sample includes the added element of Enduring Understandings (described in detail in chapter 8), because I believe they are crucial for any Jewish PBL unit.

Unit: *T'filah*

Name of Project: Personal Picture Siddur · *Grades 3 and up*

Content Area(s): *T'filah*, Hebrew, Jewish History, Technology

Enduring Understandings:
- When we understand the origins of the prayers and the reason for their order in prayer services, we gain an appreciation for and understanding of *t'filah*.
- *T'filah* creates a two-sided relationship with the Divine. *T'filah* helps us partner with God in fixing and perfecting the world.
- *T'filah* provides tools to enable us to have a transcendent experience with the Divine.
- *T'filah* is both communal and personal.
- Not all prayer is formal. There are many ways to pray/connect with God.

Key Knowledge and Success Skills:
- Learning basic prayers and the basic structure of most services.
- Decoding, translating, and practicing Hebrew.
- Examining the historical background of prayers.
- Discovering and practicing various melodies for different prayers.
- Design skills — layout, structure, etc. (older learners).

Goals:
- Students will explore their current relationship status with God and find ways to participate in that relationship (even if it doesn't seem like a relationship).
- Students will create personal prayers and find artistic connections to help them discover meaning in the formal liturgy.
- Students will investigate the order of the siddur to extrapolate meaning.

Driving Question: How can we create a more personal siddur to help us and others connect to God?

Project Summary (*Describe the student role, issue, problem, challenge, action taken, purpose/beneficiary*): Students will create a siddur that they can own, both literally and figuratively. They will explore their personal connections to *t'filah* by finding creative connections (via artwork, photography, or poetry—their own or others) with each prayer, after discovering who compiled or composed the prayer and why.

Implementation

Entry Event: Students will use their phones (or disposable cameras) or art supplies to answer one of the following questions (e.g., they can make collages from magazine images). The whole class can use the same question, or each student can decide which question to answer. Students can only use images to convey their responses—no text. Afterward, students can share their images and see how others interpret their answers. Encourage students to ask questions about both the original question and the "answers" from others.

- What would be your ideal prayer experience?
- If you could only pray by using a picture, what would that image be?
- How can humans explain what is in our deepest hearts?

Have many different versions of a siddur that students can leaf through and determine what is helpful and what is off-putting about each one. Eventually, this will lead students to the Driving Question.

Sustained Inquiry: Students will analyze the prayer service and prayers through sources such as other *sidduri*m and online Judaic learning sites, as well as delving into their own personal understandings. Students will use the Lenses of Questioning method for each prayer.

Student Voice and Choice: Students will decide what kind of artwork, photography, or poetry they will include, as well as the name of the siddur. Students will also decide which charity should receive proceeds of siddur sales. Students will create working schedules for their groups.

Reflection: Build time into schedule for students to exchange information and reflect on and assess their progress, both individually and as groups.

Critique and Revision: As students are creating content, you and their peers will critique and help them revise the content. Guide students in an interactive lesson (including text study and role-play) on giving and receiving good feedback, using Jewish sources as a basis for the lesson.

Authentic Public Product(s): A working siddur with the basic prayer services for Kabbalat Shabbat and Ma'ariv (for Shabbat). Each prayer is interwoven with artwork/photography that students either create or find. May also include poetic interpretations of prayers.

How will the product(s) be made public? Make copies of each student's siddur (or every group's version of the siddur if doing it in teams) available to the whole congregation during a family Shabbat service. Then the *siddurim* will go on sale to the general public to raise money for a cause that students choose.

Resources Needed: Art or photography supplies, computer(s), printer, many different *siddurim*.

Schedule: Depends on class. After Entry Event, put students in groups of two to four to make a group siddur, or to guide each other through the process if they are creating individual *siddurim*. Students should create roles for each person in the group, and a schedule (if they are older). Younger students need more structure and guidance.

9

Project Based Learning Plan (with Enduring Understandings)

UNIT:

NAME OF PROJECT:

Content Area(s):

Enduring Understandings:

Key Knowledge and Skills:

Goals:

Driving Question:

Project Summary (*What is the student role, issue, problem, challenge, action taken, purpose/beneficiary?*):

IMPLEMENTATION

Entry Event:

Sustained Inquiry:

Student Voice and Choice:

Reflection:

Critique and Revision:

Authentic Public Product(s):

How will the product(s) be made public?

Resources needed:

Schedule

Modern Solutions to Traditional Challenges ▶ 10

Blending Your Class

Over the years, I've encountered variations of the following students. I've worked hard to come up with creative solutions to their situations. But as technology progressed, I learned about blended classrooms and found new ways to help.

***Jennifer** is an active fifth grader. She enjoys her religious school program, although she usually misses one session a week during the fall because she also plays soccer, which is very important to her. She has fallen behind the other students because of her regular absences.*

***Daniel** is a kind and quiet fourth grader. He barely speaks during his Hebrew classes at his day school, mostly because he just doesn't understand. He is too shy to ask the teacher to slow down or repeat herself. The teacher adores Daniel. She wants to honor his shyness and not make him feel uncomfortable, but she finds it difficult to assess whether Daniel is keeping up with the material in class.*

***Ben and Eve** are seventh-grade twins. In addition to class time, they each meet with their b'nei mitzvah tutor once a week. Ben feels confident about his d'var Torah but is struggling with the trope for the Haftarah. Eve has nailed her part of the Haftarah but could use* *extra time with her tutor to learn about her Torah portion and how to construct and give a speech.*

Jack *is a high school student at a day school who loves science and math, but gets bored when reading texts and books about history. He thinks he might enjoy his Jewish history class—if it were more active and relevant to his life.*

Brianna *is a creative, passionate Jewish educator, frustrated by the limitations of time in her twice-a-week classes. She wants to involve students in engaging activities but also teach as much content as possible.*

One of the biggest challenges in the Jewish educational world is finding time to teach content and still have time for all the hands-on, exciting activities. Blended learning can help.

⬡ A Little Educational Philosophy

Many educators in the secular world use technology to help deliver content, at least some of the time. Instructors of lecture-heavy classes, especially math and science, turn to technology to engage students in ways that are hard to replicate in real life, such as virtual lab environments. They also use technology to deliver content before class, posting prerecorded videos for students to review as advance preparation. In-class time can then be used for the practice part of the work, as well as discussions and activities, such as debates, that can otherwise compete for time with content delivery. Technology also helps students who are often absent keep up with the material being taught, even though they may miss out on important in-class practice, discussions, or activities.

While we in the Jewish educational world may have a different structure to our lessons—very few are lecture-driven in the same way—technology opens the door for our students to access content, learn, play, and practice in any place, at any time. It's valuable—and the information sticks—when it solves a need.

Blended learning supports student learning with content and instruction delivered in a combination of face-to-face and digital media, both in and out of the classroom. Blended learning helps educators guide students using a variety of integrated approaches. One important goal of blended learning is to give students some element of control over the time, path, pace, or even place of their learning.

There are many variations of blended learning, the most pertinent and easily accessible of which is called the Rotation Model. In this model, students cycle between different modes, such as small-group or full-class instruction, group projects, individual tutoring, pencil-and-paper assignments—and online learning. The students learn mostly in a brick-and-mortar school setting, except for some engaging activities, which are often done at home.

Two key subsets of the Rotation Model are:

1. **Station Rotations:** Students experience the Rotation Model, as described above, but all within a contained classroom or group of classrooms. This is ideal in learning environments that don't assign any at-home practice.

2. **Flipped Learning:** Students participate in digital learning offsite in place of traditional homework and then attend the brick-and-mortar school for face-to-face, teacher-guided practice or projects. The primary delivery of content and instruction is digital, which differentiates a Flipped Classroom from students who are merely doing homework practice online at night. In **Modified Flipped Learning**, content and instruction are primarily delivered digitally, but during class time.[1]

Let's explore how blended learning and the Rotation Model can help you meet your students' learning needs.

◆ Practical Tools

Technology offers a variety of learning tools: at-home learning, smartphone and tablet apps, in-class digital programs and videos, enhanced reality. The possibilities are ever evolving—quickly.

If you are not comfortable with technology, know that you are not alone. Start slowly and focus first on the needs of your students, not any specific technology. Once you begin to identify their needs or challenges and possible solutions, then consider technology as one tool in your arsenal. Choose blended learning tools that deliver the solutions your school needs. As with any technology-based approach, the tools—whether videos, websites, or digital games—are just a means of achieving objectives, not the objectives themselves.

Whether you decide to use Flipped Learning or a Station Rotations model for an occasional lesson or for every class period, keep the focus on the overall educational goals of each lesson. If you're uneasy about technology, let your students help you— many of them have the expertise. They can find usable digital material, once you identify content, or they can make videos, for example. Even some young students can mentor those of us nondigital natives.

If your goal is to free up more class time to delve deeper into the lesson and practice skills with more one-to-one assistance, Flipped Learning can help you meet that goal by delivering content outside the class. Conversely, delivering material during class via technology (Station Rotations) can afford you more individualized and differentiated learning opportunities.

10

TIP

Video is one digital tool you can use in blended learning environments to introduce content, whether viewed together as a group or individually on students' own devices. When students watch on their own, they can't and don't tune out as easily, especially if the videos are interactive and include engaging, open-ended questions. Also, students struggling to understand a concept can always go back and replay it or pause to take notes or to ask you a question privately, thus sparing a shy student embarrassment.

Where to get video content for blended learning environments?

Produce Your Own Videos: If you are somewhat comfortable in front of a camera; have a smartphone, computer, or tablet; and can be creative and engaging, producing your own videos is a great option, especially for Hebrew and *Tanach* teachers or those teaching a skill based on information-heavy curriculum. Teachers who are natural storytellers or who want to use a lot of visuals for younger students can create their own videos to great success. (If this doesn't sound like you, skip ahead to "Use Existing Videos.")

To produce simple videos, you really only need a smartphone. More advanced tech folks might use a computer or tablet, webcam, or screencasting program such as Camtasia or Explain Everything. Screencasting programs allow you to mix a recording of yourself with other videos, visuals, and Jewish texts (source sheets can easily be found or made using Sefaria.org); and also write on a simulated whiteboard area. The goal is to keep videos engaging.

Use Existing Videos: There are many videos available on a variety of topics that students can watch and digest. Bimbam.com offers animated content on holidays, texts, life-cycle events, and more. Jewishfoodforthought.com has animated videos on Jewish ethical themes and philosophical musings. YouTube houses a variety of Hebrew language, Jewish history, and Jewish philosophy videos of varying quality, including a vast, inspiring collection by Rabbi Joe Hirsch on his channel called "The Flipped Classroom."

Most videos on YouTube and other sites can be reused. For those that don't allow reuse, try asking the person who created it to change their settings and allow you to use it for educational purposes. It has worked for me!

Create Interactive Videos: Using easy-to-follow tutorials on platforms such as Playposit.com and Edpuzzle.com, you can add original content, questions, directions, or comments to pre-existing videos. You can see which students have watched the video, and how they respond, adding accountability. Interactive videos also have built-in capabilities for formative assessments.

RESOURCE

Behrman House's Online Learning Center is a specifically Jewish platform available for blended learning. This free digital service, which can be used in class or at home, allows schools and educators to organize lessons, help students build skills with games, share ideas, and create multimedia experiences. Students can access music, videos, games, and exercises online before, after, or even during class. Teachers can post videos, downloadable PDFs, and even listen to student recordings and offer feedback.

COMMON CHALLENGES, AND SOLUTIONS

There is no one-size-fits-all approach when it comes to anything educational, technology included. Needs in your school will be driven by your specific objectives and your unique families, students, and staff.

Here are some examples of common challenges and how blended learning, in particular Station Rotations and Flipped Learning, can provide tools to address those challenges.

Challenge: Not Enough Class Time to Accomplish Everything

Technology offers a way to break up content delivery and analysis, maximizing in-person time for tasks and activities that most benefit from being together. Consider having students watch short videos on their own time, which most students enjoy, to save classroom time for meaningful applications of content that will help them connect on a more lasting level.

Here's an example of how to structure a text-based class, where students may be working on their translation skills, but you also want them to delve into the deeper meanings of the text and don't have enough class time for both.

Before class, on their own time, have students watch a five-minute video offering insight into or understanding of the text they'll be studying. During class:

1. Have students work in learning pairs (*chevruta*) to translate the text. You can circulate and help those who need extra support.

2. Then initiate a discussion based on the text and the assigned video.

3. Do an activity that helps students connect with the text and deepen their understanding, using a game (chapter 2) or Text Activator (chapter 3).

 NOTE
Adding open-ended questions to a video, using one of the sites mentioned above, can give students a platform to prepare great questions and share insights at the next in-person session.

10

Here's another example, specifically for younger students in congregational schools. Teachers spend a lot of time on the mechanics of prayer (decoding, learning tunes, and so on), without time to delve into the deeper meanings of prayers and help students make personal connections. Consider using full software packages that allow students to click and read along with the words of the prayer and record themselves saying or singing along, either in class or at home, leaving precious together time for engaging with the message of the prayer. Students who already know the prayer can begin an activity to help them connect to it personally, while others continue drilling with the software. Either way, by allowing the students to learn the mechanics via technology, it frees up the teacher and the time for other educational opportunities.

Challenge: B'nei Mitzvah Preparation

Many schools already use digital media, whether free or paid programs, to help students learn the prayers and trope. Engaging students via technology on the meatier issues, such as the philosophical ideas found within the Torah, can make a big difference in their level of engagement with the content. Tutors and teachers can create interactive videos for their b'nei mitzvah students that challenge them to come up with strong questions and answers. Having students wrestle with the content on their own can lead to more fruitful discussions when meeting with their teachers face-to-face, which in turn will lead to powerful *d'vrei Torah*. Even finding good videos to show novice or nervous students about how to give a speech or how to speak in front of an audience can help alleviate some of their anxiety.

Challenge: Programs That Don't Usually Assign Homework

For congregational schools, digital media offers an opportunity to rethink what constitutes homework. Whether it's a video game to learn Hebrew, interactive subscription-based software like iTalAm, or creating a Minecraft game walking around the Second Temple, offering students a way to engage with something fun means that they will want to do it outside of class.

There are also ways to use technology during class to engage students. Use short (three- to five-minute) videos or online content at the beginning of class to preview the main material of a lesson. This can help focus students at the beginning of class and allow late students to catch up. For example, introduce, via video (such as Bimbam.com), a section of text or *parashah* that will be examined further in the lesson. Then get students to start generating questions about the video and engage each other in discussion (see chapter 1). For advanced students, assign on online essay to read or podcast to listen to.

Another example: For a Hebrew class at any level, introduce new letters, words, constructions, or dialogue with digital games and videos (either ones you've made or preexisting). Then you can focus on individual students while other students move to the next lesson or level, or review past lessons or levels.

Challenge: Improving Student Skills

Students who are struggling, or advanced students who need additional challenge, ought to have extra practice, whether in or out of class. This could mean access to digital reinforcement materials—websites, apps, MP3s, videos, etc.

For example, videos of content taught in class can assist students struggling to understand a concept or master a skill, such as decoding Hebrew. Students can review the content as much as needed and at the pace they require. Interactive videos with assessment questions alert teachers to students who do not understand the content, so that they can give the students special attention in those areas.

For students who are outside the group norm, whether they need to extend their learning, advance, or catch up, game-style digital media can also be a great solution.

Challenge: Learners with Diverse Skill Levels and Interests

In every educational setting students' abilities and personal interests vary so much that trying to satisfy all learners can be difficult. The Station Rotations model can vary the media and content to reflect student needs and preferences. Using videos, games, and interactive formats, such as apps, give students more control over their pacing and interests.

How does this work in a class setting? With almost any subject you teach, you can create stations where some students are working on skills, some are engaging in a small-group activity, and some are independently exploring (with guidance from you) Jewish topics of interest or corollaries to that topic.

For example, some students might be working at a Hebrew station playing an online Hebrew game, others may be learning about a Jewish holiday from an interactive video, and those at a third station may be practicing singing Adon Olam, either live or following along with an audio track.

When students engage in topics that interest them, they can then share what they have learned with the rest of the class. For example, in a unit about Shabbat, a student with an interest in music could listen to online audio or videos clips of different versions of L'cha Dodi. She might pick one or two, learn them, then teach them to the class. A student interested in drawing could research online different artists' depictions of Shabbat. After studying the various works, he could come up with an original idea and share his creation with the class. Each student can complete the work for each station over the course of several class periods, allowing them to learn at their own pace and feel that they have mastered a station before moving on.

• • •

Blended learning can be used in conjunction with many other techniques and methodologies. Remember, it shouldn't feel like you're using digital media simply for the sake of using technology. Tech tools can provide flexibility in both time and media. Which platform or type of technology you use isn't necessarily important. What counts is your reason for turning to technology and how it can help you meet your and your students' needs.

As you consider the many ways to help ease time pressures, differentiate learning, and provide content to absent students, Station Rotations and Flipped Learning may be two more tools to try.

10

Experiencing Jewish Experiential Learning ▶11

It's Not Just for Summer Camp

When I started teaching, I began a tradition that continues to this day—inviting my students over for Shabbat dinner. There is something particularly memorable for students when they engage in the Shabbat rituals, eat delicious food, and sing with their teacher. I always make sure to invite a lot of my friends, too, so my students can have the opportunity to discuss important and interesting ideas with nonparent or teacher grown-ups, and celebrate a positive Jewish experience. Former students vividly remember these shared dinners. Many of them have gone on to engage more fully in Jewish life as a direct result of coming to my house for Shabbat, attending my traditional wedding, or participating in a late-night Shavuot/cheesecake learning session.

There are many transformational experiences that occur outside a classroom, whether at Jewish summer camps or retreats, on Israel trips or other tours, or in Jewish youth groups. All of these offer informal Jewish educational programming. How can we create meaningful experiences like these inside the classroom or in school settings?

Experiential Learning (or Experiential Education), like Project Based Learning, is an often misused, misunderstood term. It is an approach in which educators, as a means to deeper learning, purposefully engage with students through direct experiences and focused reflection. Because the heart of Judaism is doing, not just believing, Experiential Jewish Education (EJE) offers an engaging way to explore any mitzvah, concept, or theme.

⬢ A Little Educational Philosophy

"We will do and we will hear" (*Na'aseh v'nishma*), from the book of Exodus (24:7), is often translated as, "We will do and we will understand." In other words, if we first do what is in the Torah, we will come to understand it. From an educational standpoint, this makes a lot of sense. Full immersion in an experience is a strong path to understanding.

As Dr. Bill Robinson, dean of the William Davidson Graduate School of Jewish Education of the Jewish Theological Seminary, strongly suggests: "Education happens best—actually education only truly works—when it exists in real and tactile relation with a lived experience toward which one is being educated."[1]

In the classroom, we can craft experiences that allow students to engage emotionally with texts, rituals, Jewish history, and even Hebrew language skills. Experiential Education makes a perfect entry event in a Project Based Learning unit (see chapter 9), as a Text Activator activity to promote meaningful connectivity to a text (chapter 3), or in a storytelling milieu (chapter 7).

Professor Joseph Reimer and Dr. David Bryfman, two of the earliest authorities on EJE, explain in an essay in *What We Now Know About Jewish Education: Perspectives on Research for Practice* that three components distinguish successful EJE. Each must be present for a Jewish experience to fully facilitate learning, growth, and development.[2] Those elements are:

1. **Recreation:** Experiential Jewish Education aims to provide its participants with comfort, fun, and belonging in a Jewish context.

2. **Socialization:** Experiential Jewish Education aims to provide participants with the knowledge, skills, and attitudes to be an active member of the Jewish community.

3. **Challenge:** As Jewish experiential educators, we aim to encourage participants to stretch themselves and immerse more fully in Jewish life.

To which I would add a fourth key element essential to EJE:

4. **Reflection:** As we engage in or complete any educational experience, we should offer participants an opportunity to reflect on it in a meaningful way.

Practical Tools

Before you begin planning an experience, just as with all lessons, clearly define your goals and the understandings you want students to explore. Build in some time at the end for students to reflect on the experience, whether through discussion or a creative reaction. This endpiece solidifies students' experiences and gives you an opportunity to adjust and refine the experience for the future, based on students' reactions.

The following is a themed list of EJE ideas to inspire you. All are meant for classroom or other formal educational settings, although many can certainly be adapted for camps and youth groups. Some may work better in a supplemental school; others in a day school. Two examples below highlight how the experience incorporates all four essential EJE components. Keep them in mind as you plan your own Jewish experiences.

SHABBAT AND HOLIDAYS

Shabbat Challah Baking

If you have access to a kitchen, baking challah is a great way to accomplish many educational goals: Experience the mitzvah of *hafrashat challah* (described below), explore the mystical ideas and symbolic meanings of bread, learn to recite Hamotzi, and examine the many references to bread in the Torah, all while enjoying the communal activity of baking challah together.

1. **Recreation:** Baking is an enjoyable activity to bring students together in a way that allows for relaxed and fun exchanges.

2. **Socialization:** Not only does baking together create teamwork, but baking challah adds to the sense of belonging to the Jewish people, who have been baking challah for thousands of years.

3. **Challenge:** The first challenge is in making the challah itself. Beyond that, teachers can ask questions about what bread might symbolize, and discuss the mystical and textual references while waiting for the dough to rise. The class can also learn about and perform the mitzvah of *hafrashat challah* ("taking challah," separating a small piece of dough, which we do not eat, from the rest, symbolizing the portion of dough that was given to the priests in the Temple. Even though in modern times we refer to the braided loaves as challah, the term actually refers to this small uneaten piece).

4. **Reflection:** While enjoying a taste of their labors, students can write a reflection about their experience and what they learned, in a decorated card to give to their parents with their challah as a gift for Shabbat.

11

Tashlich Field Trip

Take students to the nearest body of water to perform *tashlich* (casting out our sins symbolically with bread) shortly after Rosh Hashanah. Your educational goals might include exposing students to an interesting Jewish ritual, helping students connect with the theme of bettering ourselves during the Days of Awe, or finding comfort in rituals.

1. **Recreation:** Field trips break down the constraints of the classroom and show that learning can happen anywhere.

2. **Socialization:** This custom, as so many do, connects students to each other and the Jewish people. If you go to a public place, ask students how they feel about performing this unusual ritual with a group of Jews among non-Jews who may be in the same place.

3. **Challenge:** Have students brainstorm beforehand about what they want to cast away. Create a "cheat sheet" so they can focus intently on it as they are casting away the bread.

4. **Reflection:** Have students review their cheat sheet and reflect on whether they think the "casting out" will work. Have them think about symbolic acts in general: Why do we do them? What other symbolic acts do we do as Jews? As citizens of our country? This can be an informal discussion as they enjoy a picnic snack waterside.

Rosh Hashanah Interview

This experience is based on the idea that Rosh Hashanah is like a year-end review between an employee and the boss. Students prepare for their reviews, filling out a self-reflection form (create a template) about their strengths and weaknesses, areas in which they'd like to improve, and accomplishments from the past year. Having students dress up nicely—to impress their employer—adds to the drama! Students meet with one of the boss's assistants (a great way to incorporate older students) to review the form and together make a concrete plan of action for success in the coming year. Place each of the assistants in a different room or at workstations around a larger room. Younger students can dictate their self-reflections to the assistants. Students can take home their action plans in time for Rosh Hashanah.

Yom Kippur and a Clean Slate

Have students bring in an old coat with a lot of pockets or an empty backpack, as well as a lot of bags with handles. Then have them write with a marker on various size stones (that you bring in) some of the things they did that year that represent poor choices. The size of the stone they pick should correspond to how "big" they think the bad choice (*cheit*) was. For example, cheating on a test might be a really big rock, whereas taking an extra chocolate chip cookie when mom wasn't looking might be smaller. As they finish writing on each rock, have them add it to a bag (for big rocks) or their coat pockets or the backpack (for smaller stones). Have students walk around while wearing the coat or backpack and carrying the bags. As they add more and more rocks to their pockets and bags, it starts to weigh them down. As they are weighted down, discuss this image of Yom Kippur:

All year long we weigh ourselves down more and more with the not-so-great choices we make and the problematic things we have done. But on Yom Kippur, when we sincerely ask for forgiveness and promise to try hard not to repeat our mistakes, God lovingly turns us upside down, gives us a little shake, and all the rocks and pebbles fall out.

Have students put down their bags and empty their pockets or backpacks, putting all the stones from the whole class in a pile. Then have students pick up the empty bags and wear the lighter coats and walk around. How does it feel? Are they ready for a new year? What will they do differently in the coming year?

Chanukah and Creating Light

One beautiful idea about Chanukah is that during the darkest time of the year we bring in light. The Chanukah menorah's lights symbolize miracles, but they were miracles that required the partnership of human faith and effort with the Divine. In this experience, students make candles together for their own Chanukahh menorahs (if you want, they can even create menorahs while learning about what makes a menorah usable for Chanukah), along with extra candles to hand out to others (perhaps in a public place), with kind notes attached. In this way students can help bring light in the darkness. After handing out the candles with their notes, students can gather to reflect on the experience while enjoying *sufganiyot* (donuts).

Tu BiShevat

Beyond planting trees as an experience, creating and participating in a Tu BiShevat seder can be very meaningful. Older students can research, write, and plan the seder to make it special for younger students. Or, students can plan it for their parents.

Purim

The whole holiday of Purim—from dressing up and reading the megillah, to preparing and handing out gifts of food to friends (*mishlo'ach manot*) and gifts to the poor (*matanot la'evyonim*)—is one huge Experiential-Learning opportunity. Students can design and create fun-themed *mishlo'ach manot* to sell at a Purim carnival, or even organize and staff the Purim carnival for younger students. Then, as a class have them reflect on a Jewish cause that has a connection to Purim (they can be creative in making the connection; it doesn't have to be literal) and donate the money they make from the sales of the *mishlo'ach manot*, which helps them fulfill the mitzvah of *matanot la'evyonim* while helping others fulfill the mitzvah of *mishlo'ach manot*.

11

Passover and the Search for Chameitz

Have students write traits that they would like to "free themselves from" on pieces of paper and attach them to small chunks of bread. Hide the bread around the classroom or building. As students search in teams for their *chameitz* (the items that they want to free themselves from), they can use the traditional candle for seeking and a feather and wooden spoon for scooping up the bread. During the search, ask students to reflect on the difference between candlelight and other sources of light. See if they can find connections to why we might use candlelight. As they are scooping, ask about why we might use a feather to scoop up our *chameitz* (that which we want to get rid of). Why don't we use something solid? As they find their *chameitz*, let them scoop it into a bag. If possible, burn all the *chameitz* outside. What does it feel like to get rid of that trait or problem?

Shavuot

Late-night learning has become the tradition in many communities. Let teens try to stay up all night. Provide different stations to keep things moving, including some physical activities, and, of course, cheesecake. For younger students, have a special late-night learning (until nine o'clock or so) and pizza session. Because of the way the Jewish calendar falls, school is often out before Shavuot, but this is perfect for youth groups.

MITZVOT

Doing *mitzvot* is inherently experiential, so take advantage of that, and have students divide into groups or pairs and pick ten *mitzvot* they want to try to do for a month. Alternately, they can pick one a week for ten weeks, or for younger students, try a couple over the course of a term. Make sure they pick *mitzvot* that they don't currently do regularly. Learn about the chosen *mitzvot* as a class, or have their group do (guided) independent research. Here are some questions to consider:

- What are the laws concerning each mitzvah?
- Where is this mitzvah mentioned in the texts?
- What are the spiritual connections to the mitzvah?
- What are the challenges to keeping this mitzvah in the modern world?

Some *mitzvot* are overwhelming in their entirety for people who have never done them—like keeping Shabbat or keeping kosher. Have students try one aspect perhaps, such as lighting Shabbat candles, saying the Kiddush, or giving up use of their phones for twenty-four hours; or, for keeping kosher, have them look for kosher symbols on food or try to avoid eating milk products and meat products together at the same meal.

As students experience doing the *mitzvot*, have them create a group journal, blog, vlog, or photo essay to record their thoughts, questions, concerns, and musings. If you have a class web page or social media outlet, students can post there. Young children can draw a picture journal (pictures of themselves doing each mitzvah put together as a book—at the end of the year, this can be a real keepsake!).

JEWISH HISTORY

Whether recreating moments in history, debating important issues, or simulating events or experiences, using EJE can bring Jewish history to life and clarify its relevance.

For any time period or event, focus on the main educational goals (see the lesson-planning template in chapter 16), then add the four important components of EJE: recreation, socialization, challenge, and reflection. Of course, experiences need to be engaging and allow students to connect with fellow Jews (in the case of Jewish history, Jews in a different place and time); students need time to reflect on current-day relevance. Questions for you to consider when planning and for students to discuss after the experience include:

- Why is it important to learn this?
- How does this event affect the present?
- What lessons can we learn from this event or time period?
- How does this event or time period affect us as a people (our collective psyche, how we approach the world, etc.)? Individually?

The experience should guide students to be able to answer these questions.

NOTE
Jewish history has many joyful moments as well as the painful times. When creating experiences to help students understand or connect with the more difficult events, remember to keep them age-appropriate. For example, a Holocaust simulation that proved effective for high school students might traumatize younger students.

JEWISH VALUES

Jewish values are meant to be lived. Students might better understand the merit of living a Jewish life by actually experiencing the meaning and importance of our Jewish values. Have learners explore Jewish texts that exemplify or explain these values before immersing in them.

Tzedakah

More than just charity, the root of the word tzedakah is *tzedek*, which means "justice." By immersing themselves in meaningful work for worthy organizations, students can feel that they are helping to create a more just world. Have the class choose a cause or two in which they can get involved (not just to raise money) and through which they can feel they have made a difference.

Tikun Olam

Tikun olam means "repairing the world." Students can create a *tikun olam* fair, similar to the Proverbs Fair discussed in chapter 3. Every game or activity can help educate and inspire participants—whether other students, campers, or the community at large—about important causes that help our world and the people in it. Any money collected can then be sent to those organizations.

Chesed

Have students develop a *chesed*—"loving kindness"—project that they can implement. This can be an ongoing exercise that includes a reflection journal or social media page. Even young students can think of ways to express kindness to others.

11

Hakarat Hatov

Have students decide on a person, organization, or other establishment to whom they would like to express *hakarat hatov*, or "gratitude" (especially one that isn't expecting it). Have them plan a special "Thank-You" party.

Bal Tashchit

There are many environmental issues to be addressed today. One way to demonstrate *bal tashchit* (caring for the environment)? Clean up a beach, park, or even neighborhood streets, and increase the impact and fun with a before, during, and after photo shoot (students can use their own devices, or you can provide them with disposable cameras), and some rockin' Hebrew music.

• • •

As the divide between formal and informal Jewish education blurs, we are able to cross-pollinate both areas. In the school realm, often seen as formal education, using EJE, in addition to the array of other tools, methodologies, and approaches described in this book, contributes to helping students find new understandings of what it means to be—and to do—Jewish.

Jewish Education Is a Family Affair ▶ 12

Family Programming

Most of the experiences I had as a child and a teenager that molded my Jewish identity included my family—Shabbat dinners, Soviet Jewry rallies, celebrating Israel at the JCC, and, of course, our yearly Passover seders. In the time I spent "doing Jewish" with my family, whether celebrating holidays or engaging in social action—my parents modeled for me and my siblings the importance of Judaism in our lives. My parents also taught us, by example, that learning is a lifelong process, and that at every age we have something to learn and something to teach. At the beginning of my teaching career, my mom, who is an artist, was working on a Miriam's Cup. She asked me to teach her all about Miriam, from the Torah, the commentaries, and the Midrash. How lovely to have my mom as my chevruta.

As adults, my siblings and I express our Judaism in very different ways, but we all feel the connection to our heritage and religion, and we pass that connection on to our children.

As educators, we have an opportunity to support and guide families as they, too, explore and connect to their Judaism. Family education is not just a bonus add-on in our children's Jewish education, but an essential component of any program. It does take a lot of thought, preparation, reflection, and refinement to successfully engage families with meaningful content. So, where do you begin?

Judaism has one of the most original and successful ongoing family-education programs in history. In fact, it was created about three thousand years ago and has evolved into a perennial favorite for the majority of Jews—the Passover seder. It is the perfect prototype, when done well, for family-education programs that we might run today. It has:

- **Clear goals:** We engage with the seder every year to understand, appreciate, and try to experience the Exodus from Egypt.

- **Experiential Learning:** We go through the steps of the seder and make an emotional connection to them. Some traditions, like the Syrian custom of walking around the table with a heavy pillowcase slung across one's back, or the Persian and Afghani custom of "whipping" each other (with scallions) during Dayeinu, demand that we partake in learning with our whole being.

- **Plenty of food:** The food is also part of the experience as it is symbolic and meaningful, often yummy and sometimes bitter.

- **Storytelling:** A great story goes a long way!

- **Room for creativity:** Many families have personal traditions and fun additions to the seder that make it unique and entertaining.

- **The opportunity to ask a lot of questions:** Passover seders are all about questions, and not just four of them!

- **Engagement in learning:** Many families enjoy delving into the text, sharing new insights, debating ideas, and exploring the commentaries.

- **Intergenerational involvement:** Unlike many educational programs, a seder is meant to be shared by all ages.

- **Open and accessible to all types of learners:** All four types of "children" are welcome, and the learning is scaffolded accordingly, each to his or her needs.

- **Singing:** When people sing together, something special happens!

This is a terrific checklist to consider when creating an effective, engaging family-education program or curriculum.

⬡ A Little Educational Philosophy

What is the difference between teaching secular subjects and Judaic subjects? It's pretty simple. When teachers give an advanced math class, they are teaching skills that may be useful in life to *some* of their students, but not all. I have actively used what I learned in Algebra 2 perhaps three times in my fairly long life. My teachers likely harbored no illusions that I might someday be a mathematician or scientist. When I took social sciences or English, my teachers' goal wasn't to train me to become a professional in those fields, but rather to provide a well-rounded understanding of the world—past and present. (Joke's on them, though, since I do teach English and write professionally.) But when we teach Judaic subjects, it's not just for knowledge's sake. We are training students to *be* Jewish. We are giving them the tools they need to be lifelong Jews. We are preparing them to join an extraordinary community that spans the whole world, as much as it does their neighborhood. We want them to understand that learning in Judaism is an ongoing pursuit. Unlike math or science though, students often stop learning about Judaism right after their *b'nei mitzvah*. I can't imagine thinking that I had learned everything I needed to know about English or history by the time I was thirteen. So why do so many Jewish educational programs end at the bar or bat mitzvah? How can we turn that tide? Even now I know that I haven't yet learned everything I need to know about Judaism, or education, for that matter.

The key to creating adults who appreciate and desire Jewish community, and lifelong Jewish learning and connection, is having parents model the same. Without parents creating an authentic model for their children, the chances of their children picking it up on their own are very slim. As educators, we need to help our parents become this positive model by providing ongoing, engaging programs for families that give parents the tools and motivation to build up their family's Jewish living. How can we live more Jewishly, viewing life through a Jewish lens? How would our ideal family grow from these programs? What would our ideal family look like? What do we want our families, led by the parents, to take away from their experiences? Every congregation and community has to answer these questions for themselves, and plan accordingly.

◆ Practical Tools

Family education is not "one size fits all"; there are many shapes and sizes. As with any educational program, learning objectives need to be examined and solidified as you begin brainstorming and planning. During this process, keep in mind the list of successful elements from our seder, and decide which ones you want to include:

- **Clear goals:** Make sure that every activity or program has clear educational goals. Also, see how you can tie in programming to your current curriculum.

- **Experiential Learning:** See chapter 11 for inspiration.

- **Plenty of food:** Cooking, baking, and eating are all great ways to bring people together.

- **Storytelling:** People of all ages love a good story.

- **Room for creativity:** Art, creative writing, filmmaking, performance, dance, and music can all bring families together for powerful experiences.

12

- **The opportunity to ask a lot of questions:** Building this into every activity or program is essential.

- **Engagement in learning:** The challenge is finding activities and programs that will appeal to different ages and interests.

- **Intergenerational involvement:** A chance for the generations to interact and learn from each other is more powerful than parents just watching a performance or observing a kid-only activity.

- **Open and accessible to all types of learners:** Parents and children may all have different learning strengths and challenges. The more we formulate our programming with layers of presentation styles, the better.

- **Singing:** When people sing together, something special happens!

There are five additional categories to consider when creating family-education experiences:

1. **Topic:** What topics do you want to explore? Does the program enhance the current curriculum? Which topics are most engaging for the families? Which are most important for your institution's families? What topics are better experienced as a family?

2. **Time Frame:** What time frame do you have available? Do you have time for a family education experience every week? Once a month? Twice a year? Consider how long each program can be: An hour? Two to three hours? All day? Are your programs time-specific, such as every Shabbat or before each holiday?

3. **Structure:** What structure or format will you be using? Do you want the learning to be self-directed or led by an educator or other facilitator? Will the families be together the entire time, or will there be times when parents are learning with other parents, while students learn together? Will families regroup before and/or after?

4. **Space:** What spaces will you be using? Your school or congregation? Are there other places where learning can happen? How will you use the spaces? What furniture do you need?

5. **Age:** What is the age range of students involved? How will you modify your approach to the content to suit diverse age groups? How will you keep all ages engaged?

TIP

Here are some other great ideas for planning successful family-education programming from Diane Zimmerman, a veteran Jewish educational leader with more than twenty-five years of experience. She is the associate educator at Temple Sinai in Washington, DC.:

- Plan time for parents to talk to each other. This might be a snack break, or a wrap-up session, or a pre-program coffee and Danish time.

- Plan for introductions—consider using "camp-style" welcoming activities as a warm-up (see chapter 13 for icebreakers).

- Make sure to have signs or clear directions, if needed, to tell people where to go as they enter.

- Provide clear communication about what is happening when, so parents understand what's expected of them and don't feel "tricked" into more learning.

- Carefully consider how you will handle children who show up without a parent—and communicate that ahead of time. For example, if you are doing a program on death and mourning in Jewish tradition, it would not appropriate for a child to be there without a parent).

- At the end of the program leave time for reflection on the learning or create a closing that ties everything together.

- Consider providing a take-home for families to remember the experience.

- Follow up afterward with an e-mail thank-you and a summary, a copy of materials, or a video to watch to reconnect. This will help parents who were not able to make it to the event to feel a little more connected (and see what they missed).

- Each experience should be part of the larger ongoing program.

FAMILY PROGRAMMING FORMATS

The following three family-programming formats—self-directed stations, facilitated stations, and round-robin learning sessions—work for a variety of family-education topics, settings and ages. Examples accompany each format.

SELF-DIRECTED STATIONS

Set up various stations throughout the building or around a large room, such as a social hall. The stations should all be very different from each other and build on the ideas that you want to convey. Every activity should have clear directions so families can move around and complete each activity at their own pace. Your content and overall objectives will determine the kinds of activities, as well as the age groups involved. And remember that your activities need to encourage and engage the parent and child to work together.

Traveling through the Year

Topic: Jewish Holidays

Time Frame: Before (or during) each holiday

Structure of the Program: Self-Directed Stations

Location/Space: Social hall and various classrooms

Ages: Parents and children grades K-6

Enduring Understandings:
- The Jewish holidays give us a meaningful vehicle for engaging with our families throughout the year.
- Celebrating Jewish holidays enriches our souls.

Learning Objectives:
Participants will:
- Create and practice using ritual objects related to each holiday that they can take home.
- Recite the appropriate blessings and sing holiday songs.
- Discover the deeper meanings of each holiday.
- Prepare and enjoy traditional holiday foods.

Other Objectives:
- Families will be able to experience the holidays together.
- Families will get to interact with other families.

The Plan: At the beginning of the year, give each family member a "passport." Stamp their passports with an appropriate holiday stamp as they visit stations at each program during the year. (If you don't have time during the school year for a family learning day for each holiday, you can do all the holidays in one day. Make a station or two for every holiday.)

Stations for a Rosh Hashanah program might include:

Apples and Honey—Practice saying the blessing then dip and eat. Try providing a variety of apples and different kinds of honey. Have a taste testing and a chart to record preferences. After eating, each person gives a "sweet" blessing to everyone for the new year (e.g., good health, not too much homework, strong friendships.

Storytelling—Storybooks pertaining to Rosh Hashanah and its themes (such as starting over, asking for forgiveness, and trying our best to be good people) fill up a table. Families can read a few out loud. Ask participants to tell a story, if they have one, that relates to the theme of the story they read. For example, a book on starting over might prompt, "Tell a story about a time that you were able to start over. How did it help you?"

Letters to Ourselves—Display various Rosh Hashanah greeting cards. Have each person write a card to him- or herself expressing wishes for the new year, all that they hope to accomplish, words of advice, and personal goals. Younger students can dictate to their parents. Everyone can draw on and decorate the cards and envelopes. Then each family puts all of their cards in one big envelope. At the final family program of the year, return the envelopes to each family.

NOTE

In the self-directed learning framework, it is important that all materials and texts are easily accessible by participants of all ages and backgrounds.

FACILITATED STATIONS

This is similar to Self-Directed Stations, but some or all of these stations' activities are led or run by facilitators, such as a teachers or teenage counselors (*madrichim*). This method is especially helpful with larger crowds.

A Trip to Israel

Topic: Israel's Geography and Special Places

Time Frame: One day

Structure of the Program: Facilitated Stations

Location/Space: Social hall and various classrooms

Ages: Parents and children grades K-8

Enduring Understandings:
- Israel is a beautiful, varied, and exciting land, with many important places and experiences for the Jewish people.
- Israel is made up of Jews from all over the world, as well as Christians, Muslims, and people of other religions.

Learning Objectives:
Participants will:
- Familiarize themselves with the various cities and major destinations in Israel.
- Enjoy Israeli experiences.
- Engage in activities that connect with Israel.
- Eat traditional Middle Eastern foods.

12

Other Objectives:
- Families will be able to connect with Israel and see it as a prime place for a family trip.
- Families will get to interact with other families.

The Plan: Each family meets with a "travel agent" to plan their journey (which stations they will be visiting and in which order, based on their preferences). Each station is a city, special attraction, or activity found in Israel, such as the *shuk* (market; which can provide food, drinks, and souvenirs made by students at an earlier date), the Kotel (Western Wall), Masada, Israeli dancing, Gaga (the game), an Eilat glass-bottomed boat, and so on.

At every station, a "tour guide" (teachers and *madrichim* in costumes) introduces the location or activity with a brief bit of background and helps facilitate the activity. Families can travel with other families while participating in the stations, which will promote great interaction.

Decorate the walls with pictures of Israelis of all backgrounds, as well as beautiful scenes from all over Israel that show off the diverse geography.

ROUND-ROBIN LEARNING SESSIONS

This format allows families to examine a piece of text together and learn from each other.

Gather parents and their kids around tables. Each family should have its own table or learning area. Distribute a short, age-appropriate text or story to study. Have the family discuss it together and come up with six questions based on the Lenses of Questioning (see chapter 1). Then have them pass their questions to the family on the right. Each family should spend five to ten minutes on the list, trying to answer at least one question. Families keep passing to the right, until the original group gets back its answers. Each group discusses. Alternatively, you can put two families together or mix and match families to create family teams. This gives people a chance to get to know one another and also gives any child whose parents are unable to attend a chance to join a "family" table.

The Story of Rabbi Zusya

Topic: Living Up to Our Potential

Time Frame: 1–1 ½ hours

Structure of the Program: Round-Robin Learning Session

Location/Space: Social hall or other larger room

Ages: Parents and teens grades 7-12. This activity would also work well with grandparents.

Enduring Understandings:

- "Who is wise? One who learns from all people" (*Pirkei Avot* 4:1).
- Learning together as a family is rewarding.
- Living up to our fullest potential is a goal for which we must constantly strive.

Learning Objectives:

Participants will:

- Analyze a piece of text.
- Engage in the learning process, including asking questions.
- Find ways of relating to the text.

Other Objectives:

- Families will experience the importance of learning together.
- Families will get to interact with and learn from other families.

The Plan: Hand out the following story:

Rabbi Zusya was on his deathbed, and tears were streaming down his face.

"Why are you crying?" asked his disciples.

"If God asks me why I wasn't like Moses or Maimonides," answered Rabbi Zusya, "I'll say that I wasn't blessed with their kind of leadership ability or wisdom. But what if God asks, 'Zusya, why weren't you more like Zusya? Why didn't you realize your potential?' That is why I am crying."

Before having families come up with questions, explain the Lenses of Questioning categories to them (if you use it in class, students will already know!) and provide at least one chart per table. You might want to give participants some examples the first time they try this activity. Then, if you meet weekly or monthly, they will be able to come up with questions on their own.

Here are some examples of Lens questions:

- **Orange:** Who is Maimonides?
- **Blue:** At what moments in your life do you feel like you've realized your inner potential?
- **Green:** How do you think Rabbi Zusya's students answered him? How might their lives have been changed by his answers to God?
- **Yellow:** When is it helpful to compare ourselves to others?
- **Gray:** What is the problem with comparing ourselves to others?
- **Red:** Why do you think Rabbi Zusya is sad?

USING ALTERNATE SPACES

The following approaches break from the traditional places of learning, proving that Jewish learning can happen anywhere.

12

Shabbaton or Retreat

Location: Any campground (available off-season) or retreat center

Whenever we engage with nature, we open ourselves up to memorable experiences and learning. A program of this magnitude takes a lot of planning, but the results can be very meaningful. Pick an overall theme, and create programs and activities that relate to that theme, revealing different aspects of it. Vary the activities between the physical and the cerebral—scavenger hunts versus Round-Robin Learning Sessions. Build in free time for participants to get to know each other and hang out together. Add a communal challah bake with music if the retreat includes a day before Shabbat.

Chavurot

Location: Various families' homes

Each session is prepared, led, and hosted by a different family, with the help of an educator or clergy. Other families come to the host family's home for activities, singing, and learning around a particular aspect of a theme that the families pick together at the beginning of the year.

Field Trips

Location: Wherever something Jewish is happening!

Are there interesting Jewish-related places in or around your community? Is there a "traditional" Jewish neighborhood nearby? Is there a Jewish-themed movie? Or even a family-friendly movie with themes worth discussing? This is a great way to create memories together as a family and community. Including time for questions, discussion, and reflection (maybe even through performance or art) really adds to the learning experience.

Judaism on the Go

This is adapted from an idea by Diane Zimmerman (see Tip, page 129), with kind permission. Judaism and learning aren't just tied to specific places and times. Judaism on the Go shows us that we can infuse our experiences with and see connections to Judaism wherever we go. There are dozens of possibilities for helping families see life through a Jewish lens. Here are two examples:

Museum Hunt

Location: Any museum in the world

While visiting a museum together, families look through a list of Jewish quotes. They then try to find a quote that matches what they are viewing. For example, if they were looking at Van Gogh's *Starry Night*, they might match it to the quote, "Please look toward heaven and count the stars, if you are able. . . So shall your offspring be" (Genesis 15:5). If the museum allows it, participants can take pictures of the art and post them with the quotes on the school or congregation website. Find quotes in the Torah, the book of Proverbs, *Pirkei Avot*, the siddur, or Jewish songs; put together a "Museum Hunt" quote sheet that can be downloaded and handed out.

Mitzvah Bingo

Location: Anywhere

Create a set of four or five Mitzvah Bingo cards that families can take on road trips and other vacations. Each board is filled with different *mitzvot*, as seen below, and of course, a "FREE" space in the middle. Every time the family witnesses or participates in one of the *mitzvot* on the board, whoever has that mitzvah gets to check it off.

Some ideas for *mitzvot* to fill the board include:

Honoring parents	Saying a blessing	Taking care of our planet	Being kind to animals	Giving charity
Mezuzah	Making challah	Returning a lost item	Loving our fellow Jews	Being kind to strangers
Honoring scholars	Being fair in business transactions	**FREE**	Giving truthful testimony	_____
_____	_____	_____	_____	_____
_____	_____	_____	_____	_____

What other mitzvot are important to your school or congregation?

This is a good activity to distribute before a school break, with a prize given to all winning Bingo boards when they return.

Shabbat Together

Locations: Various families' homes

Clergy members or teachers invite over for Shabbat dinner two to three families who live close to each other or who have children in the same grade. During the course of the dinner, families can experience some of the Shabbat traditions that the congregational community enjoys in a warm atmosphere. Alternatively, have families get together with other families to make Shabbat happen. Set up a rotating schedule for once a month or more, if your families are open to it, with different families hosting. You can send home a Do-It-Yourself kit that you create, perhaps with the help of your students, to assist the families in their preparations and celebration. Or you can make a lively video that walks families through Shabbat (include the blessings, some good recipes, and fun songs). That way, they can watch, prepare, and practice ahead of time.

OTHER FORMS OF FAMILY INVOLVEMENT

Here are some quick and easy ways to keep families involved that don't require as much planning.

Send home a question of the week—something the family can discuss. It should be an open-ended question related to what you have been learning in class. If you e-mail it, parents can type in the answer and you can post all the answers on a special page or blog on your school's web site. This has the added bonus of letting parents know what their students are learning in class and then being able to discuss it with them.

Ask students to find a Jewish artifact from their family—something that has meaning for them. Give students questions to ask their parents. Have students take a picture of the item (or bring it in if it is not too valuable) and then have a class show-and-tell with the artifacts.

Empower parents to teach their kids! Send families a short piece of text, a blessing, or other content that you want your students to know, and give the adults the tools they need to teach it to their kids. Make a video for the families or set up a blog.

● ● ●

As you review these ideas and formats, keep in mind that you know best what works for your community. Each time you try a program, reflect on it afterward. Where were the successes, and where were the challenges? How can the program be refined for future use?

Keeping families learning together is our most powerful tool in helping our students see the relevance of Judaism in their lives. Family education requires detailed planning with a focus on strong goals, but our investment can reap huge rewards.

Family Programming Planner

Topic:

Time Frame:

Structure of Program:

Location/Space:

Ages:

Enduring Understandings:

Learning Objectives:

Participants will:

Other Objectives:

The Plan:

PART FOUR

Putting It All Together: Teachers' Tools

I'll never forget a day almost twenty years ago, when I was a new teacher and came a bit unprepared to teach my sixth-grade Jewish history class, hoping I could somehow wing it. My students seemed to sense this and acted out even more than usual. As I turned to a bookshelf to look for a miracle that might present itself in the form of an idea, the room suddenly grew quiet. Strangely quiet. I turned back around to see the head of school sitting in the last row with a grin on his face; he was there for a surprise evaluation. I froze. He was very intimidating. After a few eternal seconds, I gathered myself, plucked a book from the shelf, and decided we would create a play about a section of Jewish history I had wanted to cover. The good news was that the head of school also completely intimidated my students. Thus, they behaved perfectly for the rest of class.

The head of school later sent me a note complimenting my classroom management skills. I chuckled, knowing that I actually needed some serious help in that department. He also praised my creativity in turning Jewish history into a play and engaging the students, and I felt that I was on to something. I also learned the importance of planning lessons thoughtfully and thoroughly. There was so much to think about my first year of teaching—and every year after that.

Teaching is a lot like juggling. We are trying to remember so many things while keeping all the balls in the air. We must keep everything moving, making sure that distractions don't derail us, and having to adjust when another ball is thrown at us. It's challenging! I once took a circus-skills class in college. I failed juggling.

Maybe teaching is more like . . . Well, as you know, it is like nothing else. Failures haunt us, and everyday little successes loom large. We have the capacity to change lives, inspire souls, and bring meaning to our students. But it takes a lot of work—putting together the puzzle pieces in just the right way and knowing that tomorrow the puzzle may change again. Luckily, I love puzzles.

This section provides some tools to pull everything together—to help juggle the balls, put the pieces of the puzzle together, or whatever metaphor you envision. The last chapter is on lesson planning—taking everything from the previous sections, and all that you know, and making it concrete.

In the Beginning and Beyond ▶ 13

Icebreakers and Community Makers

After leaving my film career for a new beginning as a Jewish educator, I became a student again. I came to Israel to do some learning and enrolled in a program in which I didn't know anybody. At our first session, the rabbi put many beautiful and interesting photos on the table in front of us. He then asked us to each pick a photo that especially spoke to us and explain our choice. We learned many intriguing things about each other as everyone told an interesting story, prompted by their photo. This icebreaker's impact was immediate; we got to know each other in a lovely way very quickly. Some of the people I connected with that day are still dear friends more than twenty years later.

Since then I have recreated the same activity for my various Judaic studies and English classes, but with an eclectic assortment of my own photos (I am an avid amateur photographer). I enjoy getting to know the students through their explanations and stories. After the activity, I reveal to my students that I took all of the photos. As they look at the photos again with this new information, they begin to feel a connection to me, knowing that I took the photo they chose.

Beginnings are often really hard. Starting a new class or a new job, coming to a conference or convention, even just walking into a room with people you don't know can be daunting. The Torah describes how God created order from chaos; much of it has to do with introducing elements and giving them purpose. When we begin a new class or facilitate a group, we, too, have to create order from chaos by helping introduce the elements—in this case, students or participants—to each other and giving them purpose. This is how we build community in our classrooms, youth groups, and congregations.

⬢ A Little Educational Philosophy

Successful education is all about relationships—between the teacher or facilitator and the students, between the students and each other, and between all of them and the material. To initiate and grow these relationships, we can use shortcuts to get us closer to where we want to be: These are icebreakers.

Creating community is also an essential element of a positive learning environment. Helping learners get to know and trust each other while having a fun experience fosters bonding and helps groups quickly build connections. Icebreakers provide this opportunity.

Many kinds of classroom and group situations can be enhanced with a well-thought-out icebreaker. But different situations may require different types of icebreakers. Are students new to each other and the teacher? Do the students know each other but not the teacher? Are they first graders starting the school year or adults about to embark on a weeklong mission to Israel? Is it a camp session or a weekend retreat? Is it the beginning of the year or time for reconnecting in the middle of the year? Creating clear goals will help you choose what kind of ice breaker will best meet your needs.

⬢ Practical Tools

Below is an assortment of icebreakers, many with a Jewish spin, that can be used and adapted for your programs and classes.

PHOTO INTRO

A Jewish version of the above-mentioned activity, good for all ages, in which each participant chooses a photograph from an eclectic collection.

Goal: To enable participants to share stories or other interesting parts of themselves to forge faster connections with each other and with you.

Preparation: Find and print out (on stock card is best) interesting photos with a mix of both Jewish content and not explicitly Jewish content.

The Activity: Students choose the photo with which they best connect and explain why. Ask high schoolers and adults to choose a photo they feel is a metaphor for their Jewish connection or journey.

An Alternative: Make two copies of each photo. After students pick a photo they like from one set, shuffle the other set like a deck of cards and hand them out to students. Each student looks at the photo they were dealt and finds the person with the matching one. The student dealt the photo then interviews the student who chose the same picture. You can even write some questions on the back of the card to give the interviewer ideas of what to ask. After everyone finds and interviews his or her match, you can shuffle and deal again. This is also an activity you can continue throughout the year.

NAME RHYMES

A memory helper.

Goal: To help all participants remember each other's names.

Preparation: None.

The Activity: Each person comes up with a short rhyme or alliteration for their name that gives information about him- or herself. For example, "I'm 'Love-to-Read Josh Fried.'" or "I'm 'Colorful Chloe.'" Although this may seem suitable only for younger kids, I have done this successfully with adults, and it really helps me remember people's names.

THE CINDERELLA

Adapted from Rivi Frankel, a tour guide in Israel (and my stepdaughter), who leads groups of all sizes.

Goal: To help large groups bond quickly.

Preparation: None.

The Activity: Everyone takes off his or her left shoe and throws it in a pile in the center of the room or space. Each person then takes one shoe from the assortment and has to find its owner. When they do, the shoe's owner states five Jewish things about him- or herself—Hebrew name, favorite Jewish holiday, favorite Jewish food, etc. After everyone has learned a bit about his or her "Cinderella," the person holding the shoe introduces its owner to the whole group. You can do this with as few as fifteen people and as many as seventy.

A DIFFERENT PERSPECTIVE

Also adapted from Rivi Frankel.

Goal: To help people make strong one-to-one connections and see things from the perspectives of others.

TIP

My favorite trick to learning students' names quickly? Take small wipe boards and dry erase markers and have students write their names on a board—one at a time—then hold the board by their face while you take a picture. Then at home later, flip through the pictures and test yourself until you've memorized all the names and faces (I usually just do first names, and learn their last names later). The next day, students will feel great when you know all their names.

13

Preparation: Make sure every participant has a device for taking pictures.

The Activity: The group divides into pairs. Each pair consists of an *Alef* person and a *Bet* person. The *Alef*s go out into whatever space you are in (synagogue, outdoors, etc.), and take a picture of something meaningful to them. Then the *Alef*s escort their *Bet* partners to the vicinity of where their picture was taken, and the *Bet* partner takes a picture of something around there that moves them. They compare the pictures. Were they of the same or different things? Why did they choose their photo subject? Why that particular angle? And so on.

HUMAN BINGO

A popular icebreaker, ideal for camps, youth groups, and retreats, with many possible variations.

Goal: To help participants meet as many people as possible and facilitate brief discussions.

Preparation: Make a variety of bingo cards (see the sample below). Instead of numbers on the squares, put things like: "Has been to Israel more than once," "Can speak more than two languages," "Has given tzedakah in the past week," and so on. You can also add in non-Jewish-themed squares, such as "Has two or more pets" or "Plays a sport." The cards can easily be made to reflect the ages and potential experiences of each class or group. Be sure to bring pens and prizes.

The Activity: Each participant gets a Human Bingo card and a pen. Everybody circulates, finding people who fulfill each square in a row (or any other version you choose, such as an X or even the whole card). Each person writes his or her name or initials in the box. To make it more challenging for older players, tell them they can't ask anything directly; they must find a way to fit it into conversation. Offer prizes for the first few bingos.

Sample Human Bingo card:

Was born in New York	Loves playing games on handheld devices	Has visited more than four states	Has celebrated Passover in another country
Has been to a Jewish wedding	Can blow a shofar	Has read every Harry Potter book	Flew a kite in in the last year
Gave tzedakah in the past month	Can tell the time in another language	Has family of Middle Eastern descent	Has a last name of fewer than four letters
Has more than one pet	Has visited Israel	Plays an instrument	Has a baseball-card collection

TREASURE HUNT

More preparation, big payoff.

Goal: To help participants become familiar with each other while exploring a new location—the synagogue, campground, a Jewish neighborhood, etc.

Preparation: Make clues that lead teams from one location to another with clever wordplay or puzzles. Then take a meaningful Jewish verse or text, print it out in large letters on card stock, and cut out each word. These will be the pieces of the "treasure." You'll need a copy of each clue and treasure piece for every team. Other items you will need:

- Poster board
- Glue stick
- Markers
- Scissors
- Magazines

The Activity: Divide participants into small groups of three or four (younger children can have a teacher, *madrich*, or counselor with them).

Each group, starting at a different location, finds a clue that leads to the next location AND a piece of "treasure" (place the word in an envelope, or give each team an envelope in which to keep their treasure pieces). Ensure there are enough clues and treasure pieces at each location, so that every time a group finds the spot, they can take just one clue and treasure piece, and leave the rest for the other teams. The teams are not competing against each other, so there's no need for one team to sabotage another by taking all the treasure pieces at any given place or removing the next clue.

After the groups have completed the treasure hunt and collected all the pieces of the verse, go back to a central area where you have all the supplies ready. Have each team glue the pieces of the verse onto a poster board, discuss the verse, then decorate the poster with markers and images cut from magazines to express what they think the verse means or how it relates to their lives. They can then present their posters to the larger group.

THE WHOLE PICTURE

Perfect for mixed-age groups.

Goal: To provide a fun way for people of various ages and backgrounds to meet and interact. It is especially good for groups of forty or more, including families or multi-grade retreats.

Preparation: Print out beautiful or interesting photos (of Israel, of Jewish rituals, or whatever is appropriate) on card stock. Cut each picture into a puzzle (about eight to ten pieces per photo). You will need at least one photo puzzle for every eight to ten people. You will need to know ahead of time exactly how many are in

NOTE

You can make a different treasure packet for each group, with lines that create a prayer or a series of verses from the Torah or *Pirkei Avot*. It is more work, and the treasure for each group would need to be identifiable at each location, but in the end, each team will be contributing to a group treasure.

13

the class or group with which you are working.

The Activity: As each person enters the room, hand them a puzzle piece that helps create one of the puzzles in this activity. Then have them find the rest of the pieces (and the people who go with them) of their puzzle. The first group to complete their puzzle wins.

MAKING CONNECTIONS

A great icebreaker for larger groups of any age.

Goal: To help large groups connect in a quick and fun way by showing what they have in common, and to provide great conversation starters as people get to know each other after the activity.

Preparation: Gather chairs in a circle.

The Activity: Everybody sits in a circle. One person (often the teacher or facilitator, who also plays) stands in the center and says something about him- or herself like, "I am a Denver Broncos fan." If someone else is a Denver Broncos Fan, they can stand up and say, "I'm a Denver Broncos Fan, too." They come to the center, and the first person sits down. The second person shares a new fact about him- or herself, such as, "My bat mitzvah parashah was *Bereishit* (Genesis)." If no one has a connection, the person in the middle has to come up with a new statement and try again. The facilitator can also call, "Close enough!" and someone can find a tangential connection. For example, when the person says, "I'm a Denver Broncos Fan," the facilitator can call "close enough!" and someone can stand up and say, "I lived in Denver once" or "I like watching football." They would then go to the middle. Try to get everyone in the middle at least once. Or let everyone go only once.

THE INTERVIEW

A verbal game that bypasses formal introductions. Grades 3 and up.

Goal: To help participants who will spend a significantly long period of time with each other (students, bunkmates, committee members, etc.) quickly learn about each other.

Preparation: You will need:
- Sheets of paper
- Pens or pencils
- A few suggestions for questions

The Activity: Give each person a sheet of paper and a pen or pencil. Ask participants to write down no more than four questions that they would ask someone they were trying to get to know. At least two questions should be Jewishly oriented. For example, eighth graders at a camp might ask, "What was the highlight of your bar/bat mitzvah, if you had one?" Young kids at a school might ask, "What is your favorite Jewish holiday and why?" Adults might ask, "What was your most powerful Jewish experience?" Tell them to steer clear of obvious questions like, "What's your name?" "What's your favorite color?" or "What do you do?" (for adults).

After they have written down their questions, have everyone start mingling and exchanging answers with as many new people as possible. Allow about ten minutes for this icebreaker, then have each participant stand up and say his or her name aloud, one at a time. As each person says their name, everyone else shouts out something they found out about that person during question time. Allow as many as five facts to surface about each person.

Encourage every member of the group to chip in with "facts," while ensuring that every member of the group gets a turn to say his or her name. If no one remembers anything about a particular person, ask that person to answer his or her own questions.

TOO MANY COOKS

A good way for people to accomplish something together, and you can finish with cooking. Bonding over shared food—what could be more Jewish?

Goal: To facilitate discussion and teamwork in smaller groups as participants get to know each other.

Preparation: Cut recipes of simple Jewish/Israeli/Middle Eastern dishes (from a variety of countries) into strips. Every recipe should be separated, so that the title, every ingredient, and each step of the directions is on separate strip of paper. Then put all the pieces to each recipe into an envelope. You will need a different recipe for each team of three to six people. Bring small prizes if you are rewarding the winning group.

The Activity: Begin by having each team introduce themselves to each other. Tell each team:
- Each member of the group will receive part of recipe (an ingredient, direction, etc.).
- Your job is to put the recipe in order as quickly as possible so that it makes sense.
- When your group is done, loudly announce *b'tei'avon!* (bon appétit) to signal the end of the game.

Allow ten to twelve minutes for the game. Once a team calls *b'tei'avon!* have them introduce themselves to the other teams and read their recipe in order.

Optional: Have the teams make their recipes and then eat together.

13

JEWISH GENIE

A nontraditional icebreaker that leads to meaningful discussions.

Goal: To provide an opportunity for deeper interaction and discussion as participants get to know each other.

Preparation: You will need:
- Flip-chart paper or giant Post-it Notes
- Markers

The Activity: Divide participants into groups of three to five people, and give each group a piece of flip-chart paper or a giant Post-it Note and a marker.

Tell participants: You and your group have just found a lamp. You rub it, and surprise! A Jewish genie appears. The genie grants you three wishes, but each wish must be from one of the following categories:
- Something you would wish for the Jewish people
- Something you would wish for the world
- Something you would wish for yourselves

Once participants have their materials, have them design wish lists for the genie. Post finished lists on a wall. The groups can then present their lists.

• • •

As you plan which icebreakers to use, think about the size of your group, their ages, the location, and your preparation time, as well as any special needs of participants. Don't forget to consider your role as facilitator. What will you do if the activity doesn't go as planned? Do you have a backup plan, or will you take a more active role in guiding your participants?

Icebreakers can set a positive tone as you begin your time together. Finding fun and interesting ways to build your community helps learners feel safe and open to new experiences.

NOTE

Many of these activities can be used not only at the beginning of the school year, but also throughout the year to build your classroom or group community. Some of them, such as "Treasure Hunt" and "A Different Perspective," can also be adapted as learning activities by connecting them to the content you are exploring.

Building ▶ 14
Relationships

Classroom Management and More

At the beginning of my career, the head of my school preferred that we use a reward system for classroom management. As a middle school teacher, I had to be creative in coming up with an effective system. Within a few months, I had it down and was pretty impressed that I could more or less control the hormonal madness. Then I switched schools. Suddenly, my foolproof method wasn't. My awesome rewards didn't motivate my new seventh-grade students. As I got to know them and what they needed, I realized I could combine my sense of humor, which we shared, with a structure that provided consequences, which they needed. What ensued was "Evil Watch"—one of my all-time-favorite classroom-management methods (explanation below). For five years, my students were so easy to manage. Until I moved to the East Coast and had to find new ways to connect and build relationships to help my class run smoothly.

As a teacher who has taught in almost every kind of educational setting— day schools, congregational schools, and youth groups of all Jewish denominations—I say with full confidence that the most important part of classroom management is building respectful relationships with and between your students. A learning environment that takes into consideration who your students are and where they are, not only as students, but also as Jews, is crucial for successful classrooms. There is no single classroom management technique that works in all situations, because educational communities and the students themselves are so different. That is why we first have to work on getting to know who our students are, and letting them get to know us. In this chapter, we will examine how to build relationships to support the goal of creating an enjoyable and meaningful learning environment for all. Additionally, there are many tips and tricks for helping create a classroom that enables and enhances learning with minimal interruptions.

⬡ A Little Educational Philosophy

Classroom management in the Jewish educational world may not at first seem significantly different from the secular-school realm. But we have strong Jewish values that we strive to communicate to our students, such as behaving with *derech eretz* (literally, "the way of the land," but more commonly understood as respect), not engaging in *lashon hara* (literally, "evil speech", but refers to gossip), and *v'ahavta l'rei'acha kamocha* (loving our friend or neighbor as ourselves, Leviticus 19:18). The most successful way to relate these critical Jewish ideas and others is by building bonds and modeling the behaviors we want to see in our students in and out of the classroom.

In order to grow our relationships with our students and successfully engage them in learning Jewish values, we must make sure they feel comfortable in our safe and fair learning environment, and let them know that we are prepared and in charge. It often starts with a smile. Just showing our students how happy we are to be with them, and how passionately we care about our subject, goes a long way toward creating that welcoming atmosphere that is just as important in the middle and end of the year as it is in the beginning.

Think about your own personal teaching philosophy. How do you see your students, and how do you want them to see you? Then communicate this feeling and philosophy to your students early on. Every action you take and the way you interact with your students should reflect and amplify it.[1]

Building community is also paramount for administrators, directors, heads of school, and clergy. Students feel important when we take the time to get to know their names and something about them. Greeting them—and the parents or people who drop them off—at the beginning of the learning session sets a positive, communal tone, just as teachers greeting students by name as they come into a learning space sets a warm tone for the class.

⬡ Practical Tools

What do you want to convey to your students? What are your expectations of them? How do you visualize your ideal classroom? How much chaos can you tolerate? How will you communicate with parents, and how often? When you consider these questions, you can begin to put together a game plan for building a strong classroom.

Every class is different, even in the same school. Every year you have new students and need to establish caring relationships with those students. Keep the parents involved as much as possible, too. Here are some tips and ideas for creating an enjoyable and well-managed classroom.

AT THE BEGINNING OF THE YEAR

This is the most crucial time to begin creating your relationship with your students—to let them know who you are and what you expect of them. Consider the following:

- Think carefully about the look of your room. It should look like something great is happening there. Be careful not to over-decorate, though: Students with attention issues might find it overstimulating and distracting; students also want to know that there is a place for them to contribute. Using age-appropriate decorations is also an important consideration. Sometimes a secondary school shares space with a preschool that has already taken up the wall space. In this circumstance, consider setting up posters on easels around the room. This will let students know their class is important, too. You can also use magnets to hang up classwork on whiteboards.

- Before the first session, send a welcome e-mail to older students and to parents of younger students. Let them know a little about you and ask them to respond with information about themselves or their children. Send out a survey using a program like SurveyMonkey. Ask students' opinions about your subject, activities they enjoy, how they learn best (by listening, reading, experiencing, etc.), and so on. Let parents know how you will communicate with them. If you are tech savvy, set up a Google classroom account and create a place for students and parents to check in.

  Directors: Consider a Learning Management System that can help all of your teachers communicate with parents and students in an efficient manner, such as Alma, Schoology or the Behrman House Online Learning Center.

- For third grade and up, hand out and go over a syllabus that lets students know what they will be doing in the coming year, including topics and themes to be covered, texts and books you'll be using, skills you'll be teaching, and Essential Questions (see chapter 8) you'll be exploring. You can also include your learning and classroom expectations. At the end of your syllabus, add a tear-off section where students answer different "get-to-know-you" questions and perhaps write out some of their goals for the class.

- Ask students to help you devise three to five classroom rules that will create a great learning environment. State rules in the positive. For example, "I will listen to others respectfully and let them finish what they are saying before I speak," as opposed to, "I won't raise my hand until someone else is

14

done speaking." Another approach: "Because your classmates have so many important ideas and questions, we will give everyone a chance to share and listen carefully to others before we react." If you feel like it is appropriate to post the rules, have students create a poster. If students are mature enough, ask them to help you come up with fair consequences for broken rules. Let students know that you, too, will be following these rules. For some students, especially younger ones, it is important to review the rules for a few weeks at the beginning of the year.

- Seating charts can be useful as a means to learning names. Let students sit where they want, but have them sit in those seats for a couple of weeks. Tell them that they should let you know privately if they need to move to the front to see better or pay more attention. You can also reserve the right to change the seating if some people learn better by not sitting together. Make sure that any changes do not embarrass students in any way. Interestingly, after a couple of weeks, most students want to stay in the seats they originally chose, even when you no longer require a seating chart.

- Learn names as soon as possible (see chapter 13 on icebreakers for my favorite name-learning tip). Some teachers have an easier time of this than others. Students feel validated when you know their names.

- If you want to focus on positive reinforcement in your classroom community, open a marketplace (a shuk) of fun stuff and explain a point system. What positive behaviors get points and how many? How will you keep track of points? When will students get to shop in the shuk? At the end of each week? At the end of the month? This doesn't have to be a yearlong proposition but can be tied to the season; for example, "Elevate Yourself in Elul" points, "Chanukah *Gelt*" points, Purim points, etc.

  The prizes in the shuk don't need to cost much. The biggest prizes can be things like having Shabbat dinner with the teacher (I was surprised at how many of my sixth graders worked hard to earn points for this) or teaching the class a lesson about something of interest to them.

- Create five or so jobs in the classroom that earn students "money." You can call the money something clever or use classroom *shekels* (play Israeli money). Students fill out "applications" for the jobs they want (first and second choice), and then every few weeks you can rotate your "employees" so that everyone gets a chance. The jobs can be things like teacher's assistant, technology director, room manager (ensures room cleanliness and rule following), circulation director (hands out papers and other materials), and anything else you may need.[2] Then your students can shop in your shuk with the money they earn. For day schools, this can connect with a math unit.

- To promote a community feel, name your classroom something interesting that is Jewish or Israel related. You can come up with several names and let the students vote, or, if they are up to it, they can come up with five names and vote for the winner.

AT THE BEGINNING OF CLASS

Transitions can be tricky for many students. In congregational programs, this transition can be extra challenging because students are often trying to settle in after a long day of secular school. Here are some ideas for a smoother start. Pick something from this list, or create your own beginning-of-class routine, so students know what to expect each session. Younger students, in particular, thrive on routine.

- Play Israeli or Jewish rock/rap/reggae music (Moshav, Soulfarm, Rick Recht, Joshua Nelson, Naomi Less, Bible Raps, Matisyahu, etc.) for a few minutes at the beginning of class. When you turn it off, it's time to start learning.

- Tell a story or read from a book for five minutes (see chapter 7). This helps students of all ages settle down and focus.

- Begin the class with a quick discussion of something everyone can relate to. I once had a very squirrelly eighth-grade class full of *Doctor Who* fans. Since I am also obsessed with that TV show, I would talk with them about it for exactly five minutes at the beginning of each class (I used a timer). After our initial chat, they quieted down. Finding common ground helps build relationships with students.

- Give students a riddle or puzzle to solve that is related to something that they learned in your last session or that previews what's coming.

- Write directions on the board for a warm-up activity. When students come into the room, they read the directions and do the activity.

DURING CLASS

Keep the following suggestions in mind to engage students more fully. Doing so cuts down on the need for other forms of classroom management.

- Set the tone you want. Many teachers use humor, which is a great way to keep students focused and enjoying themselves, and opens them up to learning.

- When asking questions, randomize who gets to answer. Here's one method: Each student writes his or her name in large letters on the face of a playing card. You shuffle the deck and call on students at random. Bonus: Using cards is also a great way to sort people into pairs or groups. Because they are randomly selected, students rarely complain. I confess that I have, on occasion, set up the groups ahead of time by carefully stacking the deck in the order I wanted. It seems random to the students, but I could ensure that certain people are separated.

TIP

Before each class begins:

- Greet each student as he or she enters. If possible, stand by the door; it makes students feel welcome and a valuable member of your class community. Asking some individual questions as they get settled demonstrates that you care about them. (Say good-bye to students, by name, as they leave.)

- Post an agenda of what you will be doing during class. Sometimes I put up one cryptic item that might pique their curiosity. This has the added benefit of not having to answer the question "What are we doing today?" over and over again.

14

- Use the Lenses of Questioning technique and activities to involve everyone. Students who feel that they are an essential part of the conversation don't act out from boredom (see chapter 1).

- If everyone has a device like a phone or tablet, use a polling or quiz app like Socrative. Students can answer your questions at once, and you can monitor their answers in real time and adjust the lesson accordingly.

- Keep the lesson active. Students focus better when they get a chance to move once in a while. Create lessons that encourage some movement during the period, such as the Text Activators in chapter 3.

DISCIPLINE

When things get out of hand, a good motto to follow is:

Praise in public, discipline in private.

The second part is often hard to do, but it is important to try to avoid sending a student out of the class or yelling at him or her. Here are some ways of calming down a class and addressing other discipline problems.

When Students Have Trouble Settling Down

Try my all-time-favorite technique when students can't seem to settle down: "Evil Watch." It works when you already have a great relationship built on humor and mutual respect—and you have several minutes between class periods, recess, or time at the end of the school day. It doesn't work for every class, but I offer it up as inspiration.

Here's how it worked with my rambunctious seventh graders. I used my watch with a built-in timer and explained that it was called "Evil Watch" (again, using humor). Every time I had to wait for the class to settle down after after I had asked them once, I would look at my watch and start the timer. For every second after the first forty-five, they owed me that amount of time sitting perfectly still, in total silence. For example, if they took forty-three seconds to settle down, I did not penalize them, but if they took ninety seconds, I wrote "45 seconds" on the board, the amount of time they owed me after class. If anyone made a sound, I would start timing them all over again. In all the years I used this method, no class ever stayed after more than once or twice. Usually, all I had to do was look at my watch. Someone would shout, "Evil Watch," and they would all quiet down. We had fun with it, but one day I told them, "I have bad news and good news. The bad news is, Evil Watch died." (Cheers broke out.) "The good news is that I have a new one!" A student burst out, "Oh no! It's Evil Watch 2: Son of Evil Watch!" And that's what we called it for the rest of the year.

Even without Evil Watch (or it's evil spawn), wait for students to calm down before proceeding. Stand still and quiet and don't continue until they are ready. They may continue to try to talk and goof around, but eventually it gets awkward when the teacher stands there silently looking ahead. Eventually, they will quiet down. If students continue for more than five minutes (which might seem like an eternity), try giving instructions quietly. Contrary to what may seem obvious, speaking quietly can often work more effectively than speaking loudly. People will often quiet down to hear what you are saying.

Getting Off-Track

Allow for the occasional important digression. Sometimes the most interesting learning can happen in these situations. For example, if students ask a great question that leads to an active discussion, try to let students have their say. If digressions get out of hand, set a timer and say, "We will discuss this for five more minutes. If you don't get to have your say, you'll get two minutes to write down your thoughts and we'll put them up on the board later." If you have a Google Classroom, Facebook page, Online Learning Center class space, or blog, you can post their thoughts later with the original question. For older students, you can set up a class Twitter account that only your class can access. Instead of getting into a live conversation, give student five minutes to tweet to each other.

To avoid total derailment with questions that are way off-track, say, "That's an interesting question, but it isn't in the scope of this lesson. I'd be happy to answer it/ discuss it after class."

Give Them a Break

Sometimes when a class is losing energy or they've been working hard, I have the whole class get up and take a brain break, doing something funny, playing Simon Says (Shimon Omer in Hebrew is fun, too), or just stretching and singing "Take Me Out to the Ball Game" (extra points if it's in Hebrew!).

When Students Have Had a Hard Day

If the class as a whole has had a challenging day, say, "This wasn't your best day, but I know that you all will be great at our next session, and I can't wait to see it."

Discipline with Dignity

If a student is breaking one of your class rules or acting out, remember to discipline with dignity. Try to privately whisper to the student, or drop a note in front of him or her, saying you'd like to speak after class. If necessary, take the student out of the room to discuss the behavior.

• • •

At the end of each week, try to call or drop an e-mail to a few parents to convey something positive about their child. When students know that you acknowledge positive behavior, they often work harder to impress.

Also, be sure to share with your director or head of school what is happening in your classroom (even when it is all good). Keeping the channels of communication

14

open with administrators allows them to support you and offer suggestions. Invite them to observe so they can give clear advice. Parents and administrators are all major stakeholders in helping your students receive the best education possible. They should all be allies in this mission to build a positive learning environment. Then it will be a mission possible!

Creating Creative Assessments ▶ 15

Evidence of Learning

My first year as an educator, I taught middle-school Jewish history at a day school. There was no curriculum, and our textbooks were outdated, so most of the time I had to create my own materials. I took it to heart when the head of the school told the Judaic Studies Department that he wanted to make sure that students didn't ever feel like they were failing at being Jewish, which I translated to mean: Don't use traditional tests and quizzes. I wanted my students to have a positive experience (as we all do), and I worked hard to come up with fun and interesting ways to assess whether my students understood the material. Years later, I ran into one of my former sixth-grade students. He told me, "No teacher ever got me before. I always felt bad about myself, because I knew I was smart, but I just couldn't show it on tests. You made me feel smart and talented with all the plays and other stuff you made us do." I had achieved my goal! He didn't realize that "all the plays and other stuff" were my ways of assessing students' understanding of the material.

This chapter focuses on ways to provide evidence of learning and immediate feedback to check for understanding, whether you are a day school teacher who uses assessments regularly or a congregational teacher using them less frequently. Are students able to tie together the Big Ideas? Do students understand and know how to use and integrate the content into their lives?

⬡ A Little Educational Philosophy

Assessments are essential to the educational process. They can help motivate students to progress, aid teachers in planning future lessons, and continue to facilitate the learning process, if used correctly.

The most common assessments, of course, are tests and quizzes. These tools, although helpful in some ways, do not paint the total picture of a student's understanding, and only the most well-written tests help students apply what they have learned. Using a more creative style of assessment can help you discover the full range of knowledge students have acquired.

Creative assessments, whether formative or summative, not only provide a more comprehensive view of a student's understanding of the material, they can also give the student an opportunity to exercise critical-thinking skills. They allow students to express a range of intelligences—linguistic, logical, spatial, musical, bodily-kinesthetic, and so on. And because creative assessments furnish an enjoyable means for conveying information, students will have positive associations with their Jewish education. A well-thought-out assessment can also reinforce or further knowledge, which can be useful in any educational setting.

⬡ Practical Tools

What is a creative assessment? One that allows students to use creativity—art, music, writing, design, performance, technology—in a non-rote manner, that requires critical thinking and helps students tie together what they have learned. We don't just assess whether they comprehend the material that we have taught; we require students to use their knowledge and skills in an interesting and novel way. These kinds of assessments can also be used to reinforce knowledge and bring together all the pieces of a lesson or unit in a memorable way. Most importantly, students have to apply what they've learned.

The two kinds of assessments—formative and summative—serve different purposes, but both can be creative and challenging.

FORMATIVE ASSESSMENTS

Check-ins are an important way for a teacher to gauge student understanding before moving on to the next topic. Simply asking students if they understand or "Are there any questions?" rarely elicits a helpful response. Formative assessments aren't meant to catch students who we think weren't paying attention, but rather to help us get a sense of whether students are learning. Quizzes are currently the most often-used formative assessments, and the following examples may inspire you to move beyond them. They are perfect for all types of classes because they provide evidence of learning in an engaging way.

General Formative Assessments

Ticket to Leave: This is a popular method for quickly finding out what your students retain. You can create your own personal version, geared specifically to your subject matter, or use the following as a more general template. Leave a few minutes at the end of class for students to fill out the ticket.

Ticket to Leave

Three things I learned in today's class:

1.

2.

3.

Two questions I have:

1.

2.

One thing I would like to learn more about:

Tweet the Class: Either using a real class Twitter account or a piece of paper, have students sum up the day's lessons in 140 characters or less.

Four Corners: Pose an open-ended question about what was learned and give three possible answers. Assign one answer to each corner, leaving the fourth corner as a "Free Choice" option for students who have an altogether different answer. After students have picked their corner, have them explain why. If they chose the "Free Choice," have them share and explain their answers.

Debate a Topic: Students of every age feel empowered by being able to discuss and debate their opinions. Start by posing a question based on what you have just learned. Ask students to take sides. Younger students can simply discuss the question.

15

Content-Specific Formative Assessments

The examples below are more specific to the content being taught and ask students to find a creative way of looking at the material. This could involve role-playing, writing, songwriting, technology, art, and performance. The key is to match the assessment means with the material, not just randomly picking a modality. This takes creative thinking on your part.

If you are teaching:	Try a creative assessment like this:
The journey of the Israelites after the Exodus	Students put together a travel brochure that highlights the Israelites' trip to the Promised Land.
Maimonides's levels of giving tzedakah	Students create a 3-D art project depicting the "ladder" of levels of giving. *OR* Students perform skits showing the pros and cons of each level.
The book of Esther	Students write (younger students draw) their own *megillot*, telling the story in their own words. *OR* Students perform scenes (because a modern-day *megillah* might be a TV show) with commercials that feature products useful for each chapter (e.g., a gallows store for Haman or sleep medicine to help Ahasuerus rest at night).
The founding of the State of Israel (or any historical event)	Students publish a newspaper that tells the story from many points of view—objective reporting, editorials, letters to the editor, entertainment, sports, and so on.
The story of Deborah or Miriam	Both Deborah and Miriam are known for singing a song. Students write and perform songs that summarize their lives.
The book of Joshua	Students create a battle plan that shows they understand the unique approach that the Israelites used to conquer Jericho, circling the city and blowing the shofar. They also reflect on how Rahab and her family were saved.

Adapting Bible Stories

Whenever you are studying a story, students can take the part of different characters and be given a task to accomplish that shows they understand the narrative.

With any formative assessment, if you see that students really don't understand the material, this is the time to review it again and encourage them to try again.

Sample Creative Formative Assessments

Book of Jonah—Introduction

After reviewing Jonah 1:1-3 (God asks Jonah to go to Nineveh and get the residents to repent; Jonah decides to run away), read and discuss some of the commentaries, such as Rashi. The commentators explain Jonah's reasons for trying to flee from God's command. This short form can be used to see if students understand the ideas.

You are trying to help Jonah, who is in a great hurry to pack up and leave. He is running away from God. While rushing around, he is dictating to you all the reasons he does not want to go to Nineveh on this official complaint form.

Official Complaint Form

Submitted by: _____ (Student name)

On behalf of: Jonah

Submitted to: God

Complaint: I would rather not go to the people of Nineveh to get them
to repent for the following reasons:

Signature of Complainer: *Jonah*

Adapting for younger students: Have them role-play in pairs, with one student in charge of God's complaint department and the other as Jonah complaining about reasons he might not want to go to Nineveh. Students can switch roles. See if the new Jonah can come up with other reasons for not going to Nineveh.

Book of Jonah—Chapter 1

Students, in groups of two or three, follow the directions below to create a sea chanty or song that tells what happened on the boat from the sailors' point of view. The results are usually clever, entertaining, and informative. Each group's performance of their song also reinforces the material.

Assessment: "Sailing to Tarshish": The Sailors' Song

You were all sailors on the boat with Jonah and witnessed the terrible storm that ended with your "group conversion." In ancient times, it was customary for sailors to recount their adventures in the form of songs called "sea chantys." You are going to write and present a song that expresses all that you saw and experienced on your way to Tarshish. Include a description of the events that led to Jonah being thrown overboard and what happened to you and your fellow sailors after you threw him overboard. What did you see, think, and feel during this strange event? And, most importantly, how has your interaction with Jonah changed your life?

You can use a tune from another song or your own original tune.

15

Book of Jonah—Connection to Yom Kippur

The Book of Jonah traditionally is read on Yom Kippur and is often studied around the High Holidays. This assessment helps ensure that students understand the connection between Jonah and Yom Kippur.

Assessment: The Connection Challenge

The board of directors at your synagogue wants to make Yom Kippur more meaningful. In an effort to do so, they are debating various parts of the Yom Kippur service to see what they should emphasize. You and your committee want to make a case for highlighting the book of Jonah.

You have only ten minutes to convince the board of directors. Think up as many reasons as you can for the connection between Jonah and Yom Kippur. Make sure they're good, or it's adios to Jonah. The clock is ticking. What are you waiting for?

Our reasons for emphasizing Jonah on Yom Kippur are:

1.

2.

3.

4.

5.

SUMMATIVE ASSESSMENTS

The end of a unit of learning is time for a final, or summative, assessment. The goal of the summative assessment is to check for mastery (although for the youngest learners, the focus is as much on reinforcing concepts and tying together Big Ideas as it is on checking for understanding). While formative assessments provide an opportunity to fine-tune instruction, a summative assessment serves a different purpose. It is the culmination of a unit or topic. Creative summative assessments are excellent for differentiated learning, providing multiple ways to express comprehension and mastery.

A great way to plan a creative summative assessment is to use the GRASPS method, which comes from Understanding by Design (see chapter 8). This method fully engages students in applying the Big Ideas of a unit. By including demonstration of knowledge and skills, this is an excellent way to assess for integration with deeper understanding.

While creative assessments can take many forms, knowing what your students enjoy is a great way to reach them. For example, one year I had many students who loved to bake, so I had a Desert Dessert Challenge. They had to make a recipe that tasted great but looked like manna (a concept we had studied). Every ingredient had to tie into what we had learned about manna physically and spiritually. The dessert title had to reflect what we were learning as well. We had a panel of judges who were very happy to help out!

The key to knowing when to use GRASPS or a different kind of creative assessment really depends on the content and your learners. For example, the Desert Dessert Challenge made sense because Manna was a form of food, and my students loved baking.

GRASPS Examples

When I write an assessment, I weave in the GRASPS items in a narrative, organic way that students can more easily understand. Here are some examples:

The Last Aaron Assignment · *Grades 6-12*
The culmination of a unit on Aaron in a yearlong study of different leadership examples in Jewish text.

> **Situation:** The Jewish Leaders Hall of Fame is running out of room. They are bringing in a new exhibit about Yitzhak Rabin and are trying to decide who to take out. The director thinks they should remove the exhibit about Aaron.
>
> **Your Role:** You are a young, bright, new worker at the Jewish Leaders Hall of Fame, and you think it's a terrible idea to get rid of the Aaron exhibit. Yes, you think the exhibit is a little old-fashioned, not quite up to today's technological standards, but you are determined to prove to the director that Aaron is one of the most important leaders the Jewish people have ever had.

What You Must Do: Write a letter that will convince the director to keep Aaron. And just to make sure that there is no way the director can turn you down, you are designing a whole new exhibit—illustrations, blueprint, or diorama—to showcase how wonderful Aaron is. Make sure to include everything you know about Aaron to fully convince the director, along with an explanation of your exhibit design.

Jewish Cultural Time Travelers · *Grades 1-5*
For a class studying the culture and practices of Judaism and the synagogue.

> **Situation:** You and your time travel team, from the year 2100, have been chosen to go back in time to help your school understand more about Judaism from about a hundred years ago. Sadly, much has been forgotten.
>
> **Your Role:** It is up to your team to help the future remember important parts of Judaism.

 RESOURCE

A GRASPS refresher
- **G**oal
- **R**ole
- **A**udience
- **S**ituation
- **P**roducts or Performances
- **S**tandards and Criteria

GOAL · Provide a statement of the task. Establish the goal, problem, challenge, or obstacle in the task.

ROLE · Define the role of the students in the task. State the job of the students for the task.

AUDIENCE · Identify the target audience within the context of the scenario. Example audiences might include a client or committee.

SITUATION · Set the context of the scenario. Explain the situation.

PRODUCT · Clarify what the students will create and why they will create it.

STANDARDS · Provide students with a clear picture of success. Identify specific standards for success. Issue rubrics to the students or develop them with the students.

15

What You Must Do: Each team must bring back at least two items from each category below. When you present your findings to your school, the *[name of your school]* Jewish Academy and Space Exploration School, be prepared to explain why you picked your items and how they are used.

We are bringing the following:

- Ritual items:
- Texts:
- Articles of clothing:
- Holiday items:
- Evidence of kindness:
- Foods:
- Pictures:

Other Summative Assessments

Not every creative assessment needs to follow the GRASPS format. However, each example below provides an opportunity to use critical-thinking skills while integrating acquired knowledge, skills, and understandings. How can these ideas be adapted for your curriculum or inspire your own creativity?

Days of Creation Dance · *Grades K-2*

After learning about the seven days of Creation, have students get into seven groups or pairs. Assign each group or pair a day of Creation, and ask them to choreograph a movement that expresses what happens on that day. You might want to model the first day for them, and then have only six groups. Each group teaches their movement to the rest of the class. When you put all the movements together, the class will have made up a Days of Creation dance.

Rosh Hashanah Show-and-Tell · *Grades K-2*

After learning about Rosh Hashanah, ask students to pick an item from a table with things on it like a shofar, honey, apples, a machzor, a tzedakah box, a pomegranate, etc. Have the students pretend that they are bringing that item for show-and-tell. What do they say about it? How do they describe it?

Shabbat Blessings Stations · *Grades K-2*

This requires assistance from two other people—perhaps *madrichim*, parents, or other teachers, who will help out at the stations.

Create three stations, one with challah rolls for the blessing over challah, one with candlesticks and candles for the blessing over candles, and one with glasses of grape juice for the blessing over wine.

At each station, put a copy of the appropriate blessing in Hebrew (even if children can't read yet, it is good for them to see the Hebrew blessing), an English translation that suits your needs, and other decorations to make the station look inviting.

Divide students into three groups, assigning one to each blessing. Within each group, have some students review the blessing for the group, including any movements that go with it, while the rest of the students explain the reasons for saying that blessing. These assignments can be further broken down to include someone tasked with knowing the Hebrew (you can even break the blessing into two parts), someone tasked with knowing the motions, someone with the English, someone expressing the reasons for saying the blessing, and so on.

The students at each station then teach the rest of the class their blessing and any other information reviewed at their station. The whole class can then practice what they've learned.

Mitzvot of Abraham and Sarah · *Grades 3-5*

We learn about many important *mitzvot* when we study our foreparents—like how to greet and treat guests, visiting the sick, having faith in God—as well as many positive character traits. After students have studied a section of Abraham and Sarah's narrative and covered one or more of these important *mitzvot* or traits, have them create a pamphlet, brochure, or poster that advertises or teaches these ideas. For example, students might create "Abraham and Sarah's Guide to Greeting Guests" or "Traveling with Faith: Abram and Sarai's Guide to Going to Canaan." They may or may not come up with clever titles (or you can provide the title to get them started), but they can color, use photos cut from magazines, and write to convey content. This assessment activity can be done with other narratives as well.

The Midrash Players · *Grades 3-5*

Often we'll teach a midrash, and students will confuse it with what is actually written in the Torah. This is a good tool to check for understanding and reinforce the idea that a midrash is a story to help us understand what might seem to be missing in the narrative. Whenever you learn a section of Torah and you present a midrash, group students and have them write and perform the midrash. With older students, some groups can perform skits based on the actual text, while others perform the midrash.

Digging Deep Holiday Helper · *Grades 3-5*

For every Jewish holiday, there are deeper ideas and values to explore. An obvious example is the connection between caring for our planet and Tu BiShevat. Other examples might include forgiveness/Rosh Hashanah, *t'shuvah*/Yom Kippur, and freedom/Pesach. After your class delves into each concept, have students create their own journal collage (can include creative writing, journal entries, photographs of themselves or others engaging in the value, and other images from magazines or the Internet) for that holiday. At the end of the year, they will have a keepsake book.

Perek Packing · *Grades 5-12*

For the culmination of any book of the Bible.

Assign each pair of students one chapter (*perek*) to focus on. Have each pair plan at least seven items that they will put in their *perek* pack to represent both the literal story and any themes or ideas that were discussed. For Joshua 2, one item that students might pack, for example, would be a pair of binoculars to signify the spies (could be the real item, a miniature version, or a crafty toilet-paper-roll version). Students should also make a pack that reflects the *perek*'s story or theme.

15

For example, students focusing on the story of the Golden Calf (Exodus 32) can put everything inside a small Golden Calf.

Have each pair fill out a sheet that describes each item and why they picked it. They can use this as notes for their presentations. Students present their packs to the class in Bible order. This can be done live, or you can film students.

Bible Blogs · *Grades 7-12*

For any narrative or person in Jewish texts.

Directions: You are (name of Bible personality), and you are having a tough time. You need an outlet for your feelings and to share with the world what you are going through, so you create a blog.

1. Come up with an original name/URL address for your website/home page.

2. What would the website look like? You can load it up with pictures that reflect what is happening and what you are feeling.

3. Write what you are feeling and want to express in each post.

4. Who writes comments on your blog and what do they say?

5. Favorite links page: What sites would be on your links page (these can be real or fake sites).

6. What music/songs would be your favorites?

● ● ●

Students will rarely remember a test or quiz (and rarely fondly), but they will happily recall the activities that allowed them to express themselves, have fun, and show mastery. When you give them opportunities to tie together what they've learned and reinforce the Big Ideas through creative critical thinking, the lessons will last a lifetime.

Composing and ▶ 16
Conducting
Lesson Planning

Many longtime teachers can probably still remember the incredible challenges of that first year of teaching. If you were like me, you were stressed out and unprepared (no matter how much you prepared). Personally, I was flying by the seat of my pants, barely able to keep up. My department head always wanted lesson plans at the end of the week. I didn't really know what lesson plans were, so I would jot down a few sentences about what I thought I was going to do in class each day. I made sure to use pencil, because inevitably, by the time I had to turn in the plans, I had either not accomplished what I'd written in quick notes, or I had devised some other idea that I tried on the spot. I would then record a brief reflection on what I had done, instead of an actual lesson plan. Later, when I realized how helpful lesson plans could be, it changed my teaching completely.

After you've processed all of the other chapters in this book, with their different techniques, approaches, methodologies, and activities, it's time to put it all together.

◆ A Little Educational Philosophy

Using a lesson plan template can be a time- and class saver. The best part of making great lesson plans is that you have them for future use. After completing a lesson, reflect on how it went: Did you have enough time to accomplish your goals? Were students engaged? What were the challenges? etc. Then you can tweak, add to, and change whatever is necessary for the next time. You can also share your plan with others, whether a new teacher in your school or colleagues from other schools, so they can use your plan instead of having to reinvent the wheel. Helping other teachers raises the bar for Jewish education everywhere. Additionally, a well-written plan allows other people—such as a potential substitute—to facilitate your lesson.

⬢ Practical Tools

There are many styles of lesson plans—just search online for "Lesson-Plan Templates." But I'd like to share my template, which complements any methodology or technique. Below are the categories, with some explanation, followed by a complete sample lesson plan and a lesson-plan template.

Lesson: Name of lesson, unit, or topic.

Overview: A look at what the lesson will introduce—the big picture of the lesson or unit. This is really helpful for substitutes or others who want to know what you are covering in this lesson.

Materials: What materials will you need? This includes texts, handouts, art supplies, or anything else needed for a project or activity. As you write out your plan, you may need to add to this section, or you can highlight materials as they appear in the plan and fill in this part later.

Preparation: What do you need to do ahead of time?

Enduring Understanding(s): I always include these Big-Picture ideas. EUs are not facts; they are the accumulated wisdom that comes from examining, experiencing, and recognizing some important new idea (see chapter 8).

Essential Questions: Great open-ended questions tied into the EUs that can be used at the beginning of the unit, or throughout, to add depth to your lessons.

Skills and Knowledge: What skills and knowledge will you be focusing on for this lesson or unit?

Goals: These are the big-picture objectives that prompt inquiry, thought, and exploration of the topic. They are phrased with active verbs, expressing what we want our students to engage in and accomplish, and are usually related to our Enduring Understandings and Essential Questions.

Introduction/Set induction: For every lesson, it is really helpful to prepare students for what they're about to learn—pique their interest and hook them into your lesson. Another way to use the set induction is to review previous class material and connect it to the current lesson.

Activities: This is the main part of your lesson plan—how are you going to teach it? The more variety you can create within a block of time the better. Find different modalities of conveying information or guiding students to discover and uncover information to help them connect with the material. In this way, all will be motivated to participate and grow.

Summary/Assessments: Summarize the lesson and check for understanding. This will include evidence of learning, whether you're using formative or summative assessments. Don't forget to get creative (see chapter 15).

Reflection: After the lesson is over, write reflective notes. What were the strengths and challenges of the lesson? How can you refine it for future use?

SAMPLE LESSON PLAN

I've used this lesson for a variety of denominations, and it's appropriate for both a day school and a supplementary middle/high school.

Book of Esther: The Tables Turn

Overview: In this lesson, we will examine how everything turns around for Haman and for the Jewish people. How everything hidden becomes revealed—Esther's heritage, Haman's plot, Mordechai's heroic deed, and the ways in which God orchestrated the whole thing.

Materials: Computer and projector; two handouts: one with open-ended questions about the video and a second with text and analytical questions; article: "Seeing God in Your Rearview Mirror."[1] (The handouts that accompany this lesson plan are available at behrmanhouse.com/jec.)

Preparation: Download video about the Freedom Riders and prepare open-ended questions about how the participants in this historic event put their lives on the line for what they believed in.

Enduring Understandings:
- Some beliefs are worth fighting for and maybe even putting our lives on the line for.
- God is working behind the scenes, even when it doesn't seem obvious.

Essential Questions:
- What beliefs are worth fighting for? How far should we go to protect these beliefs?
- What are different ways God might interact in the world?

Goals—Students will:
- Be familiar with the text and narrative in Esther 5-7.
- Make connections between Esther's courage in standing up for what was right and the courage of others in history.
- Explore their own values and priorities.
- Consider different ways God works in the world.
- Analyze text.

16

Introduction/Set Induction: Start by explaining that even though we know Esther and the Jews will be fine in the end, she did not know this when she approached King Ahasuerus. She could have lost her life as well as failed to save the Jewish people.

Divide the class into pairs or threes, and give each a large Post-it Note or piece of craft paper and tape. Have each group come up with a list of at least three values or beliefs they think are worth fighting for (let groups decide what "fighting for" might entail) and write them on the large sheets of paper. Hang the sheets of paper around the room. Ask students to walk around, look at each list, and write comments on it. Do you agree? Disagree? Why or why not? How far would you go to protect these beliefs or values? Students can continue circulating around the room, engaging in further "conversations" as they add additional comments. After the activity, discuss the results: Was there any consensus? How far would some people go to protect their values or beliefs?

Activity 1: After that discussion, introduce the video about the Freedom Riders of the early 1960s. Check to see how much students already know, and fill them in on some basic details, if necessary, before showing the video.

After watching the video, discuss and compare the Freedom Riders' situation with Esther's, using the prepared questions about the video and any student questions.

Activity 2: In learning pairs, have students read through and discuss the text and answer questions on the second handout, which also asks them to write an inner monologue for Esther or Haman. (This is the formative assessment). Then review as a class. Let volunteers perform the inner monologues they wrote.

Activity 3: Hand out the article, "Seeing God in Your Rearview Mirror," and have volunteers read it out loud. Ask: How is this concept of the way in which God works related to the book of Esther? Have students pair up to discuss the potential ways God might work in the world.

Summary/Assessments: Ask students if there are any times in their lives when they can look back and see that God was orchestrating events (things we often think of as "coincidences"). Can you see God in your rearview mirror?

Reflection: The discussion in Activity 1 was fascinating but took up a lot of time. Also, need to come up with a better way to give students context for the Freedom Riders video. The inner monologues were terrific. I was surprised at how eager some of the shyer students were to perform, and the connections all the students made were varied and interesting.

• • •

Although it is often time-consuming to write down everything that we plan to do for a lesson—then rework the lesson and make notes afterward—when we do take that planning time, conduct a self-assessment, and allow our lessons to evolve, we help ourselves grow as teachers and our students to flourish.

Lesson Planner

LESSON:

Overview:

Materials:

Preparation:

Enduring Understandings:

Essential Questions:

Skills and Knowledge:

Goals:

Introduction/Set Induction:

Activity 1:

Activity 2:

Summary/Assessments:

Reflection:

PART FIVE

Shifting Paradigms: Directors and Principals Reimagining Jewish Education

Beginning when my son was a baby, my husband and I played the music we loved for him. One Shabbat evening, when he was two years old, he entertained our guests by singing all the words to "Lucy in the Sky with Diamonds." Looking on, we beamed with pride. We felt we were transmitting something lasting—our love for the Beatles and for Shabbat.

What if you wanted to introduce *your* kids or grandkids or students to the Beatles (or Michael Jackson, Mozart, musical theater, or other favorite music)? You want them to understand the depth, variety, passion, relevance, and wisdom of the Beatles' music—this music that means the world to you, that you believe will enrich their lives if only they could appreciate it.

But you will have their attention only for a short time, so you need to make some decisions: What songs will you choose to share with them? How will you optimize their attention? What setting or circumstances would be most conducive? What background information will they need? What format: audio or video? What combination of songs will make them truly appreciate the Beatles and want to hear more? What will it take to make them lifelong Beatles fans? You would probably start with the Beatles' greatest hits, because those songs are the most popular and easily accessible.

In some ways, Judaism has *its* greatest hits, too. But, just like tastes in music, what constitutes Jewish greatest hits is very personal. You have to decide what "hits"—themes, topics, texts, values, practices, customs, and so on—are the most important to convey to your students and members to help them understand the depth, passion, variety, wisdom, and relevance of Judaism. Think about what would make your Jewish greatest hits list.

Keep that list in mind throughout this section, which is primarily directed at educational leaders who want to refine their current schools and programs, or are looking for a complete, creative overhaul.

Growth and ▶ 17
Change

A Guided Process to Making Them Work

I really blew it. And I think about it all the time . . . and then let it inspire me every day!

Years ago, as the new educational director of a synagogue, I felt optimistic because I would finally be able to affect education in the way that I had hoped for when I first began this career. However, I only tried to improve the existing model instead of making radical changes. If only all that school had needed was some fine tuning. At the time, I didn't have the background, open-mindedness, tools, ideas, or courage to give the school the complete overhaul it probably needed to survive. After a frustrating year, I left to pursue other dreams. I always think about what I would do now, knowing what I know, to save that program. Alas, a year or so after I left, the school closed.

In education, not everything we try succeeds, but the knowledge we gain from our failures can motivate positive change and bring us to higher heights. Humbling experiences, such as my frustrating year at the dying school, open us up to learning more, trying harder, and, ultimately, discovering success.

Let's be honest. You've probably read too many articles about the imminent demise of Jewish education as we know it. Or you've been inspired reading about a renaissance in Jewish education. Depending on your source, it's either a lost cause or a revolution. The truth lies somewhere in between.

◆ A Little Educational Philosophy

In the world of educational philosophy, there are many passionate prophets with innovative ideas that continually challenge the status quo and open our minds to alternative approaches. The scope of the educational philosophies behind these ideas is too broad and extensive to cover in a chapter—each one requires whole books. However, it is worth investigating and studying ideas from educational pioneers such as John Dewey and Jean Piaget, Sarah Schenirer and Mordecai Kaplan, as well as from the plethora of today's educational leaders in both the secular and Jewish arenas.

Just like these leaders, we are always striving to be our best, wanting our programs to grow and improve. The process of considering change, particularly on a large scale, usually includes gathering input and approval from the various stakeholders, each with his or her own strong opinions, which may make it challenging to move forward. But open, meaningful conversations are the key to discovering whether change is even necessary, and if so, how best to implement it.

The book *Crucial Conversations: Tools for Talking When the Stakes Are High* explains, "At the core of every successful conversation lies the free flow of information. People openly and honestly express their opinions, share their feelings, and articulate their theories." This is an important step to creating a "pool of meaning," which combines each individual's input to form a larger collective intelligence that can help inform choices and provide buy-in for any future decisions.[1] These conversations can be more enjoyable and productive if we embrace some of the most honored character traits in Jewish tradition: fair-mindedness, humility, empathy, integrity, and courage.

As we survey our current school programs, consider what is working and what is not. What should we keep, and what should we revitalize or refine? How do we go about this process? And who should be involved? This chapter is meant as that starting point, the beginning of the conversation. It is a chance to prompt thinking and formulate goals.

◆ Practical Tools

What is the point of Jewish education?

This beginning point is not just an academic or theoretical question, but in fact a serious one for you to consider. Because the answer to this question lies at the very heart of the approach we take in our educational realms. For every stakeholder in your institution, the answer may be different. It's indeed a challenge to ensure that the needs and desires of the board, the clergy, the educational leaders, the teachers, the parents, and, of course, the students, are met. Asking all your stakeholders this question is a great way to gauge whether you're aligned. Where are the common points in everyone's answer? Does your program or school adequately reflect the answer to this question?

There are many ways to go about beginning conversations about potential changes with the various stakeholders. Some schools and congregations bring in consultants to help assess the situation and guide the process. Others coordinate conversations within their communities with limited or no outside help. For those doing the latter, it might be more effective and, in the long run, more efficient to have mini-meetings with each stakeholder group—for example, a group of students, the teachers, the board of directors, etc.—moderated by one or two educational leaders.

Use the following questions with each stakeholder group to begin a discussion. Aim to generate solid answers. Each group may need to meet more than once to adequately answer the questions. To streamline the process (although much spontaneous brainstorming will be missing), give group members the questions to think about ahead of time. (A blank work sheet at the end of this chapter can be used for taking notes. A downloadable copy is available at behrmanhouse.com/jec)

QUESTIONS TO CONSIDER FOR COMMUNITY ALIGNMENT

1) Who are we?

The answer to this question varies according to the group. Whom do they represent? Who are they personally? They might answer, for example, "We are the K through 8 teachers and teenage *madrichim* (assistants). We will be on the front line of implementing any changes if they are necessary." They can say their names and what they teach.

2) What do we, as a school or congregation, stand for? What values do we most identify with?

Is your organization connected to a denomination? If so, where does your school or congregation fit within the range of that denomination?

What are the principles and values you would like your program and institution to reflect and convey? This is an important list to generate. You could have everyone in the group create their own list, or work in pairs, before sharing their answers with the whole group for discussion and consolidation.

How do people from outside your congregation or school view you? Is that accurate? Is it positive?

3) What values and behavior do we want our ideal alumni to reflect?

Imagine that your current students are twenty years older. Ideally, what would they be like? How do they express their Judaism? How are they connected to the community? How are they expressing the values on your list?

Do recent alumni stay in touch? Are they reflections of what you believe in as an institution?

4) What areas of Jewish practice are important to us?

This practical question will inform much of what will be taught and modeled in your curriculum.

17

5) What are our Jewish "greatest hits"?

Go back to the introduction to Part 5 and reread it, if necessary. What are the most important aspects of Judaism that you want to convey to students? This question should generate a solid list of ten to fifteen of the most important concepts, ideas, practices, skills, and values you want students to have.

6) How would we want our students to describe the influence of our program on them?

Write up your ideal "reviews" of your program or school from former students.

Imagine students had written college application essays that express the positive effects of the Jewish education they received. What would you want them to say?

7) What skills and knowledge do we need to impart to fulfill our goals?

For each goal, greatest hit, value, and so on, what are the practical skills students must acquire?

What texts will need to be learned? What history needs to be taught? What experiences are paramount?

8) Are we mostly satisfied with the status quo? Why or why or?

If the stakeholders are fairly comfortable that the goals and values mentioned in question 2 are accurately reflected in the current program, then perhaps only a few modifications are required for continued growth and improvement. But, if most agree that there is work to be done in matching the mission with its execution, then it is time to make some big changes.

9) What are our strengths?

This is an opportunity to outline all the successes, from small to large, over the past few years. Strengths can be tangibles and intangibles, people and programs.

10) What are our challenges?

Where are all the areas of struggle? What are the obstacles to success?

This is probably the most formidable question, and honesty is paramount. Any changes being considered need to acknowledge these challenges.

11) What resources do we have?

Answers can include space, financial resources, and personnel.

12) If there were no obstacles, what would our fantasy program look like?

Imagine that financial constraints, time, and space needs were not an issue. This is an opportunity to dream big. Have the group construct their perfect program or school.

Even if the entire fantasy cannot be made real, consider what parts might be helpful and possible.

These discussions are labor intensive, but they offer an opportunity to reflect, evaluate, and dream. The next step involves bringing together representatives from each stakeholder group to present their findings and answers. This might mean gathering one board member, one clergy or other educational leader, one student, one teacher, and one parent. As you review the answers from each group representative, give time for reflection, questions, and discussion. Remember, your goal is to find common ground, and share wisdom and ideas. If the answers are wildly different from each other, that signals a need for some real soul-searching. Keep in mind the "pool of meaning" mentioned earlier.

After determining your collective goals—which may take many meetings and a lot of work—it's time to figure out what kind of changes you want to make. Copy the template on the following page or download it at behrmanhouse.com/jec. Then, let the next chapter inspire you!

17

Our Educational Vision Planner

QUESTIONS TO CONSIDER:

1. Who are we?

2. What do we stand for? What values do we most identify with?

3. What values and behavior do we want our ideal alumni to reflect?

4. What areas of Jewish practice are important to us?

5. What are our Jewish "greatest hits"?

6. How would we want our students to describe the influence of our program on them?

7. What skills and knowledge do we need to impart to fulfill our goals?

8. Are we mostly satisfied with the status quo? Why or why or?

9. What are our strengths?

10. What are our challenges?

11. What resources do we have?

12. If there were no obstacles, what would our fantasy program look like?

The Future of Jewish Education Is Now ▶ **18**

Models to Inspire

When I first decided to become a Jewish educator in the early 1990s, I was unaware of all the innovative ideas out there and the many creative and passionate educators who were already changing the face of Jewish education. In the years since, I have witnessed exciting changes and growth in programs and schools all over the country. I've enjoyed participating in the ongoing discussions about how to continue to enhance Jewish education that permeate every gathering of Jewish educators, whether at conferences, professional development meetings, or even online.

This chapter introduces innovative ideas and successes as a continuation of those conversations. The degree and quality of innovation in the Jewish educational world today is truly inspiring. After working through the questions on your "Reimagining and Enhancing Your Jewish Education Program" work sheet in chapter 17, you and your team can decide what's best for your school. Use the successes of others (and sometimes their failures) as a helpful guide. Below are some programs to inspire you; you'll find many other great examples the more you look around.

◆ Practical Tools

Perhaps you aren't interested in changing the structure of a school or program, or throwing it out and starting over with something radical (see below, if you are!).

Change does not mean a complete overhaul. Significant improvements can come from using new methodologies and tools within your existing setting and structure. Maybe that means training teachers in Jewish Experiential Learning or Flipped Learning, thus changing the whole classroom vibe. Or perhaps you'll decide to go the route of Project Based Learning, which is now at the core of many successful programs. Whatever the adjustments, it's important to make sure that the solution you seek truly aligns with the mission of the school's program. And remember, what may work for one school or class doesn't always work for another. While every school has its own strengths, unique populations, limits, and challenges, examining the successful programs of others can help to determine if and how they might work for you.

SUCCESSFUL PROGRAMS IN ACTION

Each example below begins with a brief background of the program, followed by a nuts-and-bolts section that provides some pertinent details, as well as suggestions for how it might be adapted to another school. For more information, please check the organizations' websites.

Shabbaton

Temple-Tifereth Israel, Beachwood, Ohio

Brief Background: Rabbi Richard A. Block developed Shabbaton at Beth Am in Los Altos Hills, California, and brought it along when he made the move to the suburbs of Cleveland. What is Shabbaton? It is an alternative to Sunday religious school that provides Jewish education for the whole family, giving families an opportunity to spend quality Jewish time together and create experiences that they will share and remember. Does it work? The proof is in its impact: According to Rabbi Stacy Schlein, director of education, who has continued to refine and grow the program, many of the adult alumni of the program have taken on community and synagogue leadership roles, an unforeseen but welcome byproduct. The younger students have become leaders and active members of their college Jewish communities.

Nuts and Bolts: Shabbaton meets weekly from 3:00 to 5:30 p.m. on Shabbat afternoon. Geared toward families with children in pre-K through sixth grade, Shabbaton includes adult study, grade-level cohorts, family learning, and whole-group worship and singing. Every year a major theme directs the learning and gives it focus.

For Shabbaton families with children who fall outside the pre-K to sixth-grade range, there is a separate play program for toddlers on Saturday afternoon called ShabbaTots. Older siblings (grades 7–12) serve as *madrichim* (assistants) in Shabbaton classrooms. Additionally, families get to choose between parent-child Hebrew or midweek grade-level classes, based on enrollment.

A typical Shabbaton schedule looks like this:

3:00-3:30	Service/Song Session
3:30-5:00	Adults learn with the rabbi, with time for a short snack. Each week, one of the adults leads a conversation on an area of expertise, a book they are reading, or a topic they would like to discuss together.
3:30-5:00	Children, in pre-K through sixth grade, learn within grade-level clusters. Everyone has a combination of Hebrew and Jewish studies.
5:00-5:15	All-group learning, mitzvah project, short movie, or game
5:15-5:30	Havdalah

How SHABBATON Could Be Adapted: This is a fairly simple model to adopt as an alternative to or in addition to traditional after-school/Sunday programs.

For more information: www.ttti.org

Jewish Journey Project

New York, New York

Brief Background: The Jewish Journey Project (JJP) is the vision of Rabbi Joy Levitt, executive director of JCC Manhattan, with Rabbi Lori Forman-Jacobi, director of JJP. JJP upends the traditional model of Jewish education to accommodate today's family realities, creating individualized Jewish experiences based on participants' choices. The program's overarching goal is the joyous experience of Judaism, not memorized content.

JJP serves a large number of students in New York City, and while it is very much geared toward an urban demographic, many of the ideas can be adapted for smaller cities and congregations. This model is especially ideal for a multi-congregational program.

One of JJP's keys to success is the highly talented roster of teachers, who share their passions and expertise with the goal of transmitting Jewish content. Additionally, students and their families meet with a JJP adviser to build a personal relationship. Since no two students share the exact same learning journey, every student is exposed to different content over their three or four years of participation.

Nuts and Bolts: JJP provides participants—third through seventh graders—use of the vast Jewish resources of New York City. Each JJP participant plans and builds a personalized journey, choosing courses and workshops that match his or her passions and curiosities as well as preferred mode of learning. All participants receive an online "passport" to help track their courses. Courses are grouped within pathways, or major themes of Jewish learning and living, such as:

- Hebrew
- Spirituality and Ritual
- Tikun Olam
- Jewish Peoplehood
- Torah

18

JJP's wide range of topics and modalities offers something for almost everyone. Learning experiences impart core Jewish values through an integrated approach that fuses Jewish education with other disciplines. Classes take place inside and outside of the traditional classroom. Some examples of JJP's creative and engaging classes include:

- Discovering Israel through STEAM (Science, Technology, Engineering, Arts, and Math)
- Through a Filmmaker's Lens: Diversity in Judaism
- Parsha Players
- Torah Stories and Stop Animation
- What Would You Do: Ethical Dilemmas and How to Act Jewishly
- Judaism, Animals, and Us
- Chesed Club—Doing Good for Others
- Family Book Club

Courses are offered weekly, monthly, and even during school vacations. In addition, JJP offers digital learning, including synchronous, one-on-one online Hebrew classes.

Each semester, participants travel new pathways and receive stamps on their online passports as they further their Jewish journeys. Participants track their progress throughout the semester on an interactive website and build e-portfolios that hold pictures, videos, and written entries about their JJP experiences.

JJP also partners with synagogues to offer members' children access to JJP classes. Learners who are affiliated with synagogues attend regularly scheduled "MeetUPs" at their home synagogue, in addition to their regular JJP classes, to strengthen ties between participants and their congregations. This makes JJP an ideal program for multiple congregations that want to pool resources (funds, space, educators) while maintaining individual congregants' affiliations. The strength of using JJP as the connecting program means that each congregation has autonomy in its own programming, while allowing its students to benefit from a larger range and scope of classes than each individual congregation might be able to provide.

How JJP Could Be Adapted: In larger cities, synagogues could work together to create a similar program. After-school and Sunday school programs might allow students to create their own learning journeys and use a variety of modalities of learning.

For more information: www.jewishjourneyproject.org.

JQuest
Temple Isaiah, Lafayette, California

Brief Background: In 2009, Cantor Leigh Korn and Rabbi Nicki Greninger dreamed up Shira (sing), an alternate education track for third through sixth graders to learn Jewish content through song. Shira proved such a success that the following year they added an art track, Omanut (art), cofounded by artist and parent Marcia Anderson. Because more and more students were leaving the "traditional" program to experience their Jewish learning through the specialized tracks, the school switched from its traditional program to a complete yearlong track program focused on Teva (nature track); Bonim (building track); Edot, (culture track); and Y'tzira (creation/storytelling track that includes drama, poetry and filmmaking).

Students can change tracks if they want, in keeping with JQuest's goal of honoring the idea that there are many ways to connect to Judaism and Jewish life. Each track has its own character. Like all good programming, JQuest is constantly evolving.

Nuts and Bolts: Each week, third through sixth graders attend JQuest on Sunday morning and one weekday afternoon. Tracks combine grades—third and fourth, fifth and sixth—allowing for multi-age learning. While each track focuses on different content, by the time students have completed the program, they are exposed to many different Jewish ideas and approaches.

How JQuest Could Be Adapted: Providing choices to learners brings excitement to their education. Many synagogues have already started to use this system or a modified version of it. The key to JQuest's success was a three-year transition period that began with the addition of one alternative track and slowly progressed to the complete changeover. Imagine what would happen if a day school made this bold move—offering various tracks based on students' interests. How might it affect students' enthusiasm and engagement with content?

For more information: www.temple-isaiah.org/education/kids

AND NOW FOR SOMETHING COMPLETELY DIFFERENT

Below are some ideas for more radical changes.

Change Your Space: Why does a classroom have to look like a traditional classroom? After a whole day or week of school, wouldn't students be more comfortable in a living room? Converting the classroom with couches, beanbags, comfy chairs, and a dining room-style table would entirely change the dynamic. Want a makerspace to be front and center? How about a contemplative space? A playful space? Both together?

Consider involving students in designing their ideal room. As you greet them on the first day, start in a completely empty space with blank walls, and ask them to brainstorm what would be the perfect, holy room in which to learn. Make a wish list, and ask the community for donations or look in secondhand stores. When students help create the room, they will enjoy being in it, as well as feel a sense of ownership of it and what happens in it. If a whole school takes this on, each room can have a different Jewish theme. Perhaps there are spaces like this already in your community that you can use—activity centers or museum makerspaces, etc.

Distance Learning Plus: For communities with challenges such as small Jewish populations, students who live far from the school or synagogue, or students with scheduling issues, one solution might be distance learning, with monthly Shabbat

RESOURCE

The Jewish Education Project's website, innovatingcongregations.org, provides guidance, support, and tools to help congregations make meaningful changes.

Need further inspiration and motivation for change? Read about how Temple Israel Center in White Plains, New York, created an exciting new program, Shorashim, an active, holistic approach to congregational learning, as well as other essays to give you food for thought.

RESOURCE

Make Space: How to set the Stage for Creative Collaboration, by Scott Doorley and Scott Witthoft, is a great starting point to figure out how to create your ideal space.

18

gatherings or Shabbat weekend retreats a few times a year. Online classes can be synchronous (in real time, with the teacher in one location and the students in their own homes, all sharing a virtual classroom), asynchronous (the teacher delivers content, and the students watch and respond in their own time), or a combination. This can include one-to-one online Hebrew tutoring. Then the whole community comes together for Shabbat once a month or more, to remember that Judaism is a community-centered religion. Alternatively, students could participate in a weekend retreat (*Shabbaton*) two or three times a year. This gives students a chance to create bonds with other Jewish kids, which might be especially important for families living in areas with few Jews. One Shabbaton weekend can potentially include whole families.

Community School: Many day schools already use a community model, where kids from different denominations learn together. Perhaps, in a time of dwindling memberships and school attendance, if more synagogues and temples came together and promoted cross-denominational learning, we could model for our students true *ahavat Yisrael* (the mitzvah of loving one's fellow Jews). There are already examples of this groundbreaking idea between Reform and Conservative congregations. But with the costs of Jewish day schools soaring, some in the Modern-Orthodox world are returning to public schools and looking to supplement their children's Jewish education. This might be an interesting time to bring together students from various denominations. One way to honor everyone's paths is to have some communal classes and some classes that are denomination specific. *T'filah* might be separate, for example, but storytelling or discussions on Judaic topics could be done jointly. The more opportunities we all have to get to know each other and share our thoughts and beliefs, the more we will come to understand and respect each other and the diversity of the Jewish experience. In addition, combined resources, multiple campuses, and more students allows for a creative reinterpretation of Jewish education that isn't bound by traditional issues and challenges. Successful programs include Yachad in Minneapolis (Yachadmn.org) and the Worcester Community Hebrew High School (Emanuelsinai.org/learning/hebrewhigh) in Massachusetts.

• • •

As we try new things, whether it's adjusting an existing program or making a from-the-ground-up change, don't forget the following: Keep in mind your overall goals, reflect on and assess the process, be unafraid to fail, and passionately dare to succeed. These are the keys to the growth of our programs, schools, and the Jewish future.

What's Next?

The work we do as Jewish educators may be challenging, but the rewards, of course, are great.

The more we continue to grow and learn in our craft, the greater our influence and personal satisfaction will be. So as you try out the different ideas presented here, find the combinations of approaches and methods that work best for you in your educational framework—whether that's a classroom, youth group, or camp. Here are some final ideas for putting together your own personal educator's toolbox, filled with all the tricks of the trade personalized for you:

- Create an "Education in Action" journal, which can include weekly goals, brainstorming, and reflections on lessons you taught. Commit to trying something new, and map out the steps you'll take in your journal.

- Revisit the chapters that inspired you the most. Write up ideas that you thought of or want to try out in your journal.

- Start an in-person or online learning group with fellow educators. See what other passionate educators are doing, and incorporate their successes into your own teaching practice when possible. Share your strengths and creativity with others.

- Set up a schedule of learning and sharing at staff meetings. Each educator (teachers, director, rabbi, song leader, etc.) can contribute by focusing on a chapter of "The Jewish Educator's Companion" and then leading a discussion or workshop on it.

- Form a book club with other educators based on the ideas in this book. You can find question prompts for each chapter at behrmanhouse.com/jec to help jump-start the conversation.

- Mentor and encourage new teachers. If you are a veteran educator, share the book with a colleague and include your own favorite tools and ideas.

- Find time to continue your own personal Jewish learning—an eternal and inspiring process. The more we stay connected to our passion, the more we have to give.

And finally, remember that you are part of a long and honorable tradition of Jewish educators that goes back almost four thousand years and will continue forward far into the future.

Notes

CHAPTER 1

1. Dan Rothstein and Luz Santana, "Teaching Students to Ask Their Own Questions: One Small Change Can Yield Big Results," *Harvard Education Letter* (September/October 2011): http://hepg.org/hel-home/issues/27_5/helarticle/teaching-students-to-ask-their-own-questions_507#home.

2. For more information on Six Thinking Hats, see: http://www.debonogroup.com/six_thinking_hats.php.

CHAPTER 2

1. To read the full article, see https://web.archive.org/web/20160315211834/http://www.instituteofplay.org/about/context/why-games-learning/

2. Seymour Rossel, *Managing the Jewish Classroom: How to Transform Yourself into a Master Teacher* (Los Angeles: Torah Aura, 1998), 124-126.

CHAPTER 3

Arthur W. Chickering and Zelda F. Gamson, eds. *Applying the Seven Principles for Good Practice in Undergraduate Education* (San Francisco: Jossey-Bass, 1991), 4.

CHAPTER 4

1. Eugene C. Roehlkepartain et al., *The Handbook of Spiritual Development in Childhood and Adolescence*, (Thousand Oaks, CA: Sage, 2006), 61.

2. Hannah Dreyfus, "Teaching Prayer: Obstacles, Goals, and Strategies," Kol Hamevaser (November 2011): http://www.kolhamevaser.com/2011/11/teaching-prayer-obstacles-goals-and-strategies.

3. The original curriculum was created for middle and high school to be used during a Shabbaton-type weekend experience. To read the entire curriculum, see http://www.lookstein.org/resources/experiential_tefillah.pdf.

4. Rabbi Josh Bolton, "100 Prompts, Provocations, and Situations for Jewish Growth on Campuses," *Hillel International News and Views* (blog), June 17, 2015, http://www.hillel.org/about/news-views/news-views---blog/news-and-views/2015/06/17/100-prompts-provocations-and-situations-for-jewish-growth-on-campus.

CHAPTER 5

1. Stephen Law, *The Philosophy Gym: 25 Short Adventures in Thinking* (London: Headline Review, 2004), xi.

2. Rabbi David Aaron, *The Secret Life of God: Discovering the Divine within You* (London: Shambhala, 2005), 165.

CHAPTER 6

1. Jessica Lahey, "The Benefits of Character Education: What I Learned from Teaching at a 'Core Virtues' School, *The Atlantic*, May 6, 2013: http://www.theatlantic.com/national/archive/2013/05/the-benefits-of-character-education/275585/.

2. Joel Lurie Grishaver, *You Be the Judge: A Collection of Ethical Cases and Jewish Answers* (Los Angeles: Torah Aura Productions, 2003).

3. Aviva Werner, Nathan Weiner, and Julie Botnick, *Today's Hot Topics* (Springfield, NJ: Behrman House, 2016).

14. C.Hi.P In—The Competing High Priorities Game is available at www.batshevafrankel.com.

CHAPTER 7

1. Peninnah Schram, ed., *Chosen Tales: Stories Told by Jewish Storytellers* (Northvale, NJ): Jason Aronson, 1997).

2. Annette Labovitz, "The Effectiveness of Storytelling in Jewish Education (paper presented at the Thirteenth Annual Conference of the Midwest Jewish Studies Association, Chicago, IL, January 2000). See the full paper at http://www.lookstein.org/articles/storytelling.htm.

3. Shlomo Carlebach and Susan Yael Mesinai, *Shlomo's Stories* (Northvale, NJ): Jason Aronson, 1994).

4. There are many books in the Small Miracles series by Yitta Halberstam and Judith Leventhal.

5. Peninnah Schram, *The Hungry Clothes and Other Jewish Folktales* (New York: Sterling, 2008).

CHAPTER 8

1. Jay McTighe and Elliott Seif, "A Summary of Underlying Theory and Research Base for Understanding by Design." See the full paper at: http://jaymctighe.com/wordpress/wpcontent/uploads/2011/04/UbD-Research-Base.pdf.

2. Adapted from Jay McTighe and Grant Wiggins, *Understanding by Design: Professional Development Workbook* (Alexandria, VA: Association for Supervision and Curriculum Development, 2004).

CHAPTER 9

1. Suzie Boss, *PBL for 21st Century Success* (Novato, California: Buck Institute for Education, 2013) 5.

2. To read the full article "Why Project Based Learning (PBL)?" see: http://bie.org/about/why_pbl.

3. Ibid.

4. Maayan Jaffe, "Project-based Learning Offers 'Deeper and Better' Way to Teach Judaism," *eJewish Philanthropy* (October 2015): http://ejewishphilanthropy.com/project-based-learning-offers-deeper-and-better-way-to-teach-judaism/.

5. Jessica Lahey, "To Help Students Learn, Engage the Emotions," *New York Times*, May 4, 2016, https://well.blogs.nytimes.com/2016/05/04/to-help-students-learn-engage-the-emotions/.

6. "Be kind. Be Specific. Be Helpful" is attributed to Ron Berger, renowned educator and chief academic officer for EL Education.

CHAPTER 10

1. Adapted from http://www.christenseninstitute.org/blended-learning-definitions-and-models.

CHAPTER 11

1. Dr. Bill Robinson, "Transforming Congregational Education: A Paradigm Shift," *eJewish Philanthropy* (May 2016): http://ejewishphilanthropy.com/transforming-congregational-education-a-paradigm-shift.

2. Professor Joseph Reimer and David Bryfman, "What We Know about Experiential Jewish Education." To read the full essay, see: https://bryfy.files.wordpress.com/2009/11/what-we-know-about-experiential-jewish-education.pdf.

CHAPTER 14

1. Adapted from Rebecca Mieliwocki, "Classy Classroom Management," in *What Really Works in Secondary Education*, eds. Wendy W. Murawski and Kathy Lynn Scott (Thousand Oaks, CA: Corwin, 2014), 137-149.

2. Ibid.

3. Ibid.

CHAPTER 16

Batsheva Hirschman Frankel, "Seeing God in Your Rearview Mirror," *Aish.com* (July 2005): http://www.aish.com/d/w/48944646.html.

CHAPTER 17

1. Kerry Patterson et al., *Crucial Conversations: Tools for Talking When Stakes Are High* (New York: McGraw-Hill, 2011) 20-21.

Acknowledgments

I first want to thank outstanding educator Lori Daitch for introducing me to David Behrman five years ago. It has long been my dream to work with Behrman House, and I don't know if it would have happened had Lori not made that first introduction.

Speaking of Behrman House, I am so grateful for all the love, care, and work that David, Dena Neusner, and, most especially, my main editor, Aviva Gutnick, put into this book. Aviva continually pushed me to be my best and encouraged me when I felt discouraged.

I'd like to give a special thanks to Diane Zimmerman, whose expertise on family education was invaluable to chapter 12, and whose questions, insights, and encouragement throughout the manuscript helped me focus and shape the book.

I really appreciate all of the educators who shared their stories of success and allowed me to feature their programs, ideas, and curriculum in these pages. We all learn and grow from each other! Thank you for inspiring your colleagues and helping me create a stronger book.

I am indebted to Rabbi David Aaron of Isralight and Rav Yitzchak Shurin of Yeshiva Darche Noam/Midreshet Rachel V'Chaya, as well as all of the teachers I've had from these institutions, for showing me the depths of Torah and Jewish philosophy, and supporting my goal to become a Jewish educator.

Of course, I want to thank my family. My two sets of parents have always been my biggest cheerleaders and sources of inspiration. My siblings—all of whom have taught at one time or another—have always offered love and support. My kids—the very talented and innovative educator/Israeli tour guide, Rivi, and the intuitive, loving Tuvia (who at eleven already understands what makes good teaching)—have both been helpful in so many ways. Most of all, I am so thankful to my incredible husband, whose support, love, encouragement, and caretaking allowed me to work on the book every weeknight and Sunday for the past year. It may be cliché, but it is not an overstatement to say that I couldn't have done it without him.

Lastly, I am endlessly grateful to God for bringing me along on this wild journey, guiding me each step of the way and giving me creative inspiration (that somehow usually comes to me in the shower).

About the Author

Jonah Light

Batsheva Frankel has been teaching Judaic studies, English, creative writing, and acting for more than twenty years in a diversity of places throughout Los Angeles and on the East Coast. As an educational consultant, she has given lectures, classes, and workshops at teacher conferences and schools throughout the United States and in the United Kingdom, as well as developed curricula and creative programming for a wide variety of institutions. In 2011, Batsheva began developing LaunchBox—games and activities that explore big philosophical ideas through a Jewish lens—which was the winner of the Jewish Federation of Greater Los Angeles's Next Big Jewish Idea contest. Batsheva is currently a teacher, dean of faculty, and director of community and student relations at Arete Preparatory Academy in Los Angeles.